How to Write a KILLER LinkedIn® Profile

...and 18 Mistakes to Avoid

by Brenda Bernstein, The Essay Expert

To say this book is a "Must Have" is like saying you should have a Bible.
— J. R. Hollingsworth, JD, Director of the Job Seekers Network

★ **How to Write a KILLER LinkedIn Profile is the only book we know of that is updated to the new 2019 interface!**

Here's just some of what's been changed in this new edition (14th Edition):

- Revised images and instructions throughout to match LinkedIn's new redesign
- Updates on which features have disappeared and which have moved
- New chapter on how to communicate on LinkedIn
- Chapter on LinkedIn Groups de-emphasized and moved to a Bonus Tip
- How to identify what keywords people are entering to find you **(Mistake #5)**
- How to make the most of Mutual Connections **(Mistake #5)**
- LinkedIn's new Voice Messaging & Location features **(Mistake #6)**
- The new "consecutive positions" layout **(Mistake #9)**
- Photo/video tagging and stickers **(Mistake #13)**
- Using GIFs, emojis, photos and mentions in comments **(Mistake #13)**
- Giving "Kudos" feature **(Mistake #13)**
- Sharing video updates **(Mistake #15)**
- New Jobs tools: Jobs Insights, Job Title Highlights, and Salary Highlights **(Mistake #16)**
- How to ask for a referral **(Mistake #16)**
- The new "How You Match" feature in Jobs **(Mistake #16)**
- LinkedIn Jobs' new Easy Apply option **(Mistake #16)**
- How to request a revised recommendation **(Mistake #17)**
- Updated instructions for backing up your profile **(Bonus Tip #1)**
- Updated instructions for creating a company page **(Bonus Tip #2)**
- LinkedIn's new company page Content Suggestions feature **(Bonus Tip #2)**
- Setting up two-step account verification to protect your profile **(Bonus Tip #5)**
- Revised instructions for creating a Secondary Language Profile **(Bonus Tip #7)**
- The new face of LinkedIn groups **(Bonus Tip #8)**
- Updated character limits for profile sections **(Appendix B)**
- The latest hot skills and buzzwords to avoid **(Appendix D)**
- Updated instructions on how to get free e-book updates **(Appendix G)**
- New Appendix! Setting & Privacy at-a-glance **(Appendix H)**

What's Been Discontinued

- LinkedIn Lookup
- Request an Introduction
- Conversation Starters
- Analytics for regular status updates (only analytics for Publisher articles)
- Email notifications for activity within your network
- Group activity notifications
- Group announcements
- Group job conversations
- LinkedIn Pulse
- Sharing Bookmarklet
- Old LinkedIn badges

If you have a topic, idea, or question you'd like me to address, either in the next release or on the KILLER Facebook page, go to https://theessayexpert.com/contact and tell me. I'm listening!

Appreciations

I don't know what I would have done without my Virtual Assistant, Jeanne Goodman, who has spent countless hours revising images and instructions throughout this book. She keeps me sane, able to focus on my business, and available for the speaking opportunities drummed up by my dedicated publicity guy, Scott Becher.

Brian Schwartz of SelfPublish.org, initially my publisher, continues to do a wonderful job of converting edition . . . upon edition . . . of *How to Write a KILLER LinkedIn Profile* into Kindle format.

I am particularly grateful in this 14th edition to Anne Marie Segal and Ashley Watkins, whose webinars about LinkedIn and the job search taught me valuable information that is included in this book.

Each person who has written a recommendation for me on Amazon has made my book continue to reach thousands of people who benefit in their businesses and careers.

Thank you to all of you, and to many more I did not mention, for making *How to Write a KILLER LinkedIn Profile* a longstanding success!

And thank you in advance for your generosity in considering reviewing this book on Amazon. Your support makes a difference.

Brenda

Post a review on Amazon!

How to Write a KILLER LinkedIn Profile... And 18 Mistakes to Avoid

Kindle Edition

by Brenda Bernstein ∨ (Author)

☆☆☆☆☆ ∨   347 customer reviews

› See all 2 formats and editions

Kindle	Paperback
$9.97	$24.53

Table of Contents

Bonus Tips

Appendices

Reference Links

Reviews

Within a few weeks of my complete profile overhaul, I was contacted on LinkedIn by a Director from a company completely outside of my industry. I applied for the position, which was a PERFECT fit for my skills and work style. I got the job!

— **Sara Kay**, Project Coordinator,
Los Angeles CA

I reached [the] top position for my area of expertise and location, [which led to] several offers from headhunters and CEOs. Just this month, I started a new job—and guess what? The CEO of my new company contacted me through LinkedIn!

— **Charlotte L.**, Editor,
Barcelona, Spain

I saw a sustained 4-5X traffic increase on LinkedIn by the time I was done. [My new profile] led to many new business contacts as well as an invite for an advisory board seat at a top university.

— **Joseph P.**, Board of Advisors at NJIT,
New York, NY

I got an interview within a week of implementing the changes.

— **zmyers**,
Amazon Reviewer

I used this book to improve my boss' profile and got him 20% more views.

— **Danielle**,
France

My LinkedIn rating went from 17% to 95%. I have received calls from recruiters who called after looking at my revised profile. This is a very worthwhile investment - can't recommend it enough!

— **Simon A., Writer**, Production Manager,
Vancouver, Canada

I got a job interview! I am at the top of the search function list for my industry in a 50-mile radius.

— **Matthew W.**, EMT,
Orange County, CA

I have had a 73% increase in profile views in the last week. Thank You!

— **Simon Crowther**, Project Manager,
Greater Manchester, UK

As a LinkedIn trainer myself, it's good to know I have a resource like this for my clients to help them after they've left my classroom.

— **Michael Phelps**, LinkedIn Trainer,
Little Rock, AR

About the Author

| Certified Master Resume Writer | Certified Advanced Resume Writer | Certified Executive Resume Writer | 2013 Best International Resume 2nd Place Winner | 2013 Best Sales Resume Nominee | 2012 Best New Graduate Resume 3rd Place Winner | 2012 Best Re-Entry Resume Nominee | 2011 Best Creative Resume Nominee |

Brenda Bernstein, Founder and Senior Editor at The Essay Expert LLC, is a #1 best-selling author, an in-demand speaker & consultant, and an award-winning resume writer, holding Certified Executive Resume Master and Certified Master Resume Writer certifications from Career Directors International. Her first book, *How to Write a KILLER LinkedIn® Profile*, has been featured in Fortune and Forbes Magazines; the book has consistently ranked in the top 30 in Amazon's business writing skills e-book category since July 2012. Her other e-books, *How to Write a WINNING Resume . . . 50 Tips to Reach Your Job Search Target* and *How to Write a STELLAR Executive Resume . . . 50 Tips to Reach Your Job Search Target*, have been met with rave reviews.

A top-notch editor, Brenda has 20+ years of successful written communications experience from C-level executive resume development to business copy editing and Ivy-League-bound student college essay consulting.

She holds a B.A. in English from Yale University and a J.D. from the New York University School of Law, graduating from both schools with honors. Brenda's clients report that they gain clarity about themselves and their message, in addition to having that message deliver sought-after results.

- Email: BrendaB@TheEssayExpert.com
- Web: TheEssayExpert.com / TheExecutiveExpert.com / KILLERLinkedInProfile.com
- LinkedIn: LinkedIn.com/in/brendabernstein
- Facebook: Facebook.com/TheEssayExpert
- Phone: 718-390-6696

Introduction

Why Should You Read this Book?

LinkedIn, owned by Microsoft as of the end of 2016, hosts the profiles of more than 610 million people in over 200 countries (as of April 2019). LinkedIn reports 97 million monthly unique visitors worldwide, 50% of whom are logging on via mobile devices. Furthermore, 88 of the *Fortune* 100 use LinkedIn's licensed recruiting software to search for job candidates.

Numerous studies, by entities including Microsoft, Reppler, Jobvite and Bullhorn, show convincingly that at least 97% of staffing professionals overall use LinkedIn as a recruiting tool.[1] They show further that approximately 70% of people making hiring decisions have decided NOT to hire a candidate based on what they've found on line—and that a similar percentage have hired employees based on the person's online presence. Here's the clincher: A whopping 89% of all recruiters report having hired someone through LinkedIn (as opposed to 26% from Facebook and 15% from Twitter). So if you're going to conduct a job search using social media, LinkedIn is the place to be.

Still not convinced? According to 2018-2019 research conducted by ResumeGo,[2] job applicants who have LinkedIn profiles are 71% more likely to get called in for an interview. Here are the numbers from that study:

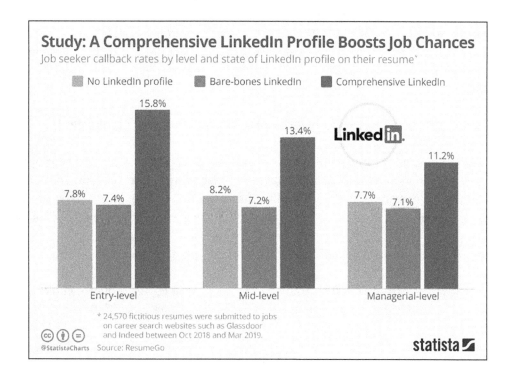

Study: A Comprehensive LinkedIn Profile Boosts Job Chances
Job seeker callback rates by level and state of LinkedIn profile on their resume*

No LinkedIn profile · Bare-bones LinkedIn · Comprehensive LinkedIn

Entry-level: 7.8% / 7.4% / 15.8%
Mid-level: 8.2% / 7.2% / 13.4%
Managerial-level: 7.7% / 7.1% / 11.2%

* 24,570 fictitious resumes were submitted to jobs on career search websites such as Glassdoor and Indeed between Oct 2018 and Mar 2019.

@StatistaCharts   Source: ResumeGo

statista

As you can see, no matter what stage of your career you're in, having a comprehensive LinkedIn profile gives you a big leg up on those either with no LinkedIn profile or with a bare-bones one. And you're actually slightly better off NOT having a LinkedIn profile than doing a half-baked job on the one you have.

Maybe you're saying "I'm not far enough along in my career" or "I'm too young." Well, LinkedIn is not just for seasoned professionals. In fact, the minimum age for membership in the U.S. is 16 (see LinkedIn's User Agreement[3]) and LinkedIn® Higher Education Pages[4] give students a place to get information about and engage in discussions with universities worldwide. If you are a high school student, now is the time to start building your network and exploring career opportunities! (See High School Students: Embrace your skills, show your professional side, and create a LinkedIn® Profile.[5]) Join the over 39 million students and recent college graduates who have already taken the leap (also see **Appendix E**).

What's crystal clear is that every single EMPLOYER or CLIENT who considers hiring you will Google you, click on your LinkedIn® profile, and assess it. Whether you are a high school or college student, job seeker, company owner or other professional, your profile MUST impress your audience if you want results from this social media treasure chest.**

Guy Kawasaki told CNBC Make It,[6] "If you're not on LinkedIn, you might as well not exist in this world. Everybody needs to be on LinkedIn."

Are you getting the results that you want from your LinkedIn profile?

If not, this book is for you. I provide you with 18 detailed strategies and writing tips, plus eight bonus tips and additional materials, that will teach you how to get found on LinkedIn, how to keep people reading and want to take action after they find you, and how to leverage this platform fully.

Using LinkedIn to its full potential can lead you to results you never imagined. Many of my clients have been amazed to get hired solely on the strength of their LinkedIn profile activity and content. I personally have built my business through the connections I've made on LinkedIn. But don't take it just from me. For more success stories, read the LinkedIn® Official Blog[7] and check out the narratives of people like account manager Sabrina Lee (Finding My Way Home on LinkedIn)[8] and digital marketer Mei Lee (My Secret Career Weapon: LinkedIn.[9])

Okay, so how will this book help you get the results you want from LinkedIn?

Since 2009, I have worked with social media experts, business people, recruiters and employers and have identified EIGHTEEN common weak points in LinkedIn profile strategy and content. These errors can be fatal if you want people not just to find your profile, but to continue reading once they do. By following the advice below, you will avoid these errors and create a frequently viewed AND highly effective LinkedIn profile.

Remember, your LinkedIn profile might never be perfect—but don't let that stop you! It's time to take action.

Use these 18 tips to create a POWERFUL profile—and show your target audience you're serious about your online presence. What's the reward? That depends on what you're looking for:

A new job . . .

An unexpected partnership . . .

A lucrative account . . .

YOU get to choose.

***Important Note on Compliance**: Some industries and companies have strict legal or corporate guidelines about what you can include in your LinkedIn profile. Nothing in this book is meant to contradict or override those guidelines. Please consult with your company and/or an attorney before making changes to your profile that might conflict with company policy or the legalities of your profession.

Important Note on LinkedIn Changes: LinkedIn changes its platform frequently. In an interview with SocialTimes, Amy Parnell, Director of User Experience at LinkedIn said, "We are in a constant state of evolution with our site and app designs, and strive to push the experience and product value to new heights on an ongoing basis."

I do my best to keep up with these changes and release new editions regularly. If you discover any outdated information in this book, rest assured that an update is on its way! Check out the Important Opportunities to Give and Receive section of this book **(Appendix J)** to read how you can get free new editions of *How to Write a KILLER LinkedIn Profile* in PDF format!

*Important Note on Tone/Non-US Profiles**: The advice in this book works no matter what country you live in. However, the tone of the samples is geared toward the United States job market. In some countries, a subtler tone might be warranted.

SECTION 1

LinkedIn Profile Nuts and Bolts

This section covers some fairly straightforward "nuts and bolts" for the "introduction card" section of your profile, including your headline, photo, websites, and public profile URL. Most of the tips in this section hold keys to being found on LinkedIn. You must have keywords that people are searching for, and you must have them in the right places. You must have a robust network of at least 500 people. You must have a photo that engages your readers. And you would be smart to get your profile to All-Star status, or something close to that!

Completing the organizations, job titles, degrees, and dates in your Experience and Education sections is also essential to having a respectable profile, but since I have not seen many profiles that don't have this information filled in, I don't address it specifically in this section.

You may want to address the items in this section before moving on and getting creative with your Summary and Experience sections. However, some people like to wait until they have a KILLER LinkedIn Profile before they start sharing it with the world, so you could opt to complete your entire profile, including your Summary, Experience and more, before building your network. It's up to you!

Mistake #1

Selling Yourself Short: Lack of Keywords and an Ineffective Headline

The Problem

There are 610+ million professionals using LinkedIn, 25% of whom are in the United States; and the site is growing exponentially with more than two new members joining every second (check out Wikipedia and these stats from Omincore[10] for more information). How will you possibly be found amongst all these people if you don't optimize your keywords? The answer is: You probably won't.

Seventy-seven percent of users[11] report that LinkedIn helps them research people and companies. When they do this research, they use keywords in LinkedIn's search box—words and phrases important to them that hopefully match the keywords in your profile. So if you want to be found as a "Sports Writer," you'll want that keyword in your profile multiple times and in the right places.

In your headline, brief titles such as "IT Consultant," "Sports Executive" or "Sales Professional" don't distinguish you from every other person with the same title in a pool of hundreds of millions of LinkedIn profiles. You must distinguish yourself in your headline to stand out, with both keywords and an attention-getting statement if possible. Otherwise you won't get to the top of LinkedIn search results and you won't capture your readers' attention.

The Tune-Up

To a certain extent, the more often a particular word or phrase shows up in your profile, the more likely it is that you will appear in people's searches when they look for that word or phrase. It's important to note that LinkedIn has a complex search algorithm. Search results are unique to the member searching for your keywords and are based in part on their profile, activity and your connections. For more on how LinkedIn's search works, see LinkedIn Search Relevance — People Search.[12]

One of the most important places to put keywords is in your Headline. The "Headline" on LinkedIn is the line under your name, and it is one of the first things people see when they look at your profile.

It might not be obvious that your zip code is a type of keyword in a way, especially if you are a job seeker. Recruiters look for job seekers by location! You will be asked to enter your zip code when you first create your account, and you must do so carefully. Adding your location makes you 23 times more likely to be found in LinkedIn searches.

The basic strategy here is to put yourself in the position of the people who are searching for you, whether they be clients, recruiters or other partners. Identify the keywords and keyword phrases they would be searching for. These keywords might include job titles, core competencies, geographical regions, technical skills, soft skills, languages and more.

If you are a job seeker, look at job advertisements for your target position and count keywords that show up repeatedly; if you like cool online tools, put the copy from a few listings into Wordle.net or WordArt.com and create a word map that shows you what words come up most frequently. Use those keywords. And—important—use a zip code that is close to the area where you want to work. If you are able to work in Chicago but live 25 miles away in the suburbs, for instance, use a zip code halfway between the two locations that will capture searches looking for someone within a 10-mile radius of either downtown Chicago or your suburb.

 Getting back to keywords: You know your profession better than anyone, so simply brainstorming commonly used words in your field can reap the perfect keywords. Here are some other ways you can find your best keywords:

- Look at profiles of other people with similar backgrounds or positions to yours.

- Use the Skills section and scan through the drop-down menus there to see what keywords LinkedIn suggests for your profession. For more about adding skills, see **Mistake #12**.

- Review job postings that interest you to see what words and phrases they're using.

- If you own a business, look at company pages of top competitors to see what language they're using.

- Follow thought leaders in your industry to see what taglines, words and phrases are trending right now.

As Catherine Byers Breet, longtime recruiter and early adopter of LinkedIn, advises, "The first hurdle is to get found (to make sure you come up in the right kind of searches by recruiters). Making sure you have industry-relevant job titles and keywords is mission-critical. If you don't, you will never come up in their searches.

Once you have identified your top keywords, add as many of them as possible in the following sections: **Headline (most important!)**, **Current Job Title**, **Summary**, and **Additional Job Titles**. The LinkedIn search tool searches entire profiles, so insert your keywords throughout! Use them early (at the beginning of your profile) and often, while keeping your language natural (i.e., don't overload to the point of offense just for the sake of keyword optimization).

Before I knew the power of keywords, my headline read: **Founder and Senior Editor, The Essay Expert.** Note the lack of keywords in that headline! Now it reads:

Brenda Bernstein

Resume & LinkedIn Profile Writer, Author, Speaker ★
Executive Resumes ★ C-Level Resumes ★ Executive LinkedIn
Profiles ★ College Essays ★ Law School Admissions Essays ★
MBA Admissions Essays

The new headline has a lot more keywords. When I changed my headline, as well as added more keywords to my Current Job Title, Summary, Specialties and other Job Titles, I went from being almost invisible in searches to coming up first in the search rankings on queries for "Executive Resume Writer" in my geographic area of Madison, WI.

Craft a headline for your profile that tells us what makes you unique and that includes as many keywords as possible. Here are some examples:

Frank Kanu • 1st

Management / Business Consultant ■ Speaker ■ Author ■
Leading Fortune 500 and Small Business Executives & Teams

Dave Stachowiak • 1st

Host, Coaching for Leaders, Top Apple & iTunes Leadership
Podcast • Senior VP, Dale Carnegie of Southern Los Angeles

Julie Van Puffelen, BSN • 1st

Epic Project Manager & Consultant | Executive Nurse Liaison |
Change Management & Support for Nursing & Ancillary Staff

Nilesh Patel • 1st

Experienced in Human Resources & Employment Law, Career
Counseling, and Nonprofit Management and Governance.

See the advantage of the above examples over headlines like "Consultant," "Senior VP" or "Project Manager"? More explicit headlines give spark and color to your profile as opposed to just listing your job title; and they contain keywords to help you appear at the top of search results. They can also hint at your personality, the results you produce, and some of your "soft skills."

> **Note:** Including proper keywords does not guarantee your profile will appear at the top of searches. There are other factors that go into search rankings, most notably your number of connections, percent profile completeness, and activity level on LinkedIn. But without keywords, your profile is guaranteed to remain at the bottom of the pile.

> **Mobile Note:** When connections search for you on their phones, your entire Headline is not visible, so use your most important keywords In the first 50 characters.

What if I've never held the position I want to be found for?

If you are seeking a position as VP of Finance, and you have never held that position before, consider creative ways of including the keywords VP and Finance. For example: VP-Level Finance Executive or Available for VP of Finance Position at Growing Company.

Of course, you need to make sure not to misrepresent yourself, so you might need to say "Poised for . . ." or something similar. Note that if you have performed the functions to match a job title, you can put the job title in your headline. I say if you've done the job, you can claim the job title! If you're a job seeker, see **Bonus Tip #4** for more about what to put in your Headline, Experience sections and updates.

Should I include a tagline?

People will get a true sense of your value if you include a tagline or "unique selling proposition" (USP) in addition to straight keywords in your headline. Best strategy: Use keywords to increase the frequency with which you are found in searches; include a tagline or USP to generate interest so people click to read more.

Once you have decided on your most effective Headline strategy, here's how to add it to your profile—and some pitfalls to avoid:

Click on the pencil icon to the right of your profile image.

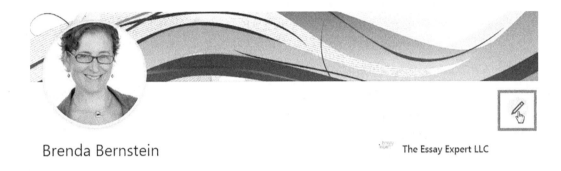

Brenda Bernstein   The Essay Expert LLC

You will then have an opportunity to edit your Headline. On the non-mobile and Android versions of LinkedIn, you have 120 characters to use.

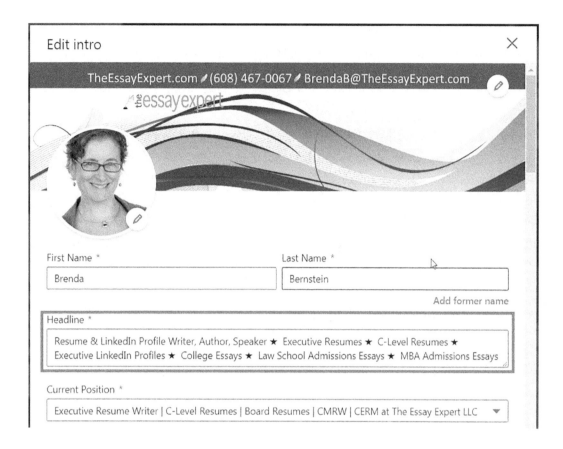

*Secret Tip: As of April 2017, unless or until LinkedIn closes this loophole, if you edit your Headline from your iOS handheld device, your characters are unlimited! However, you will have to edit your headline and summary from your phone if you go over the 120-character desktop limit.

LinkedIn will not allow you to update a profile on your desktop if the headline is too long. Remember, this trick only works on Apple® devices.

How do I include keywords in my job titles?

The job title fields are extremely important places to include keywords. Don't forget them!
Pay attention here! This is the most common tip that readers don't pay attention to and it's essential to your search rankings!!

You might think you have to put your exact job title in the "Job Title" field. You don't! You have 100 characters to play with, so use them. Put keywords in your job titles that people who are searching for you will care about. If you are a job seeker, use words that come up frequently in job descriptions for positions you want. If you are a business person, use keywords to get you found for what you do best. Here are some examples of job titles that are keyword optimized:

Example #1: Senior Legal Manager / Counsel

Senior Legal Manager - EMEA | Trusted Legal Counsel | International Deals | Compliance

Regional Senior Legal Counsel Middle East | Contract Management | Due Diligence | Project Execution

Example #2: Technology Sales Executive

Sales & Channel Account Manager, Major Accounts | Enterprise Technology | Channel Strategy

Business Development / Sales Manager | Cloud Computing | Technology Storage Sales Executive | Technology Solutions | OEM

Business / Sales Development Manager | SaaS Technology | Channel Sales Channel Sales Executive | Technology | OEM

> ****Special Note on "Keyword Stuffing"**: Some people have attempted to "stuff" keywords in their profile by adding them to their Name Field. This strategy is against LinkedIn's Terms of Service. If you have questions about what you can and can't include in the Name Field, see LinkedIn's Help Center article, Adding a Suffix or Certifications to Your Profile Name.[13]

Results to Expect

More keywords in your headline means you will rank higher in searches—*more people will find you*. And with an effective tagline, people will be sufficiently intrigued to read more. An increase in page views means more potential job inquiries or business for you. Keywords are your key to success.

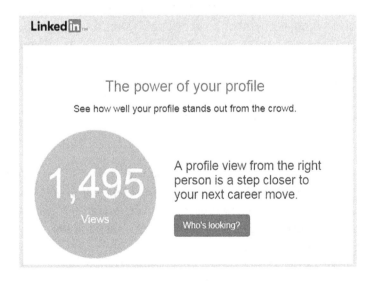

Here's an example. Let's say you have a special credential of security clearance. If someone searches for "Security Clearance" using LinkedIn's search function, something like this will appear:

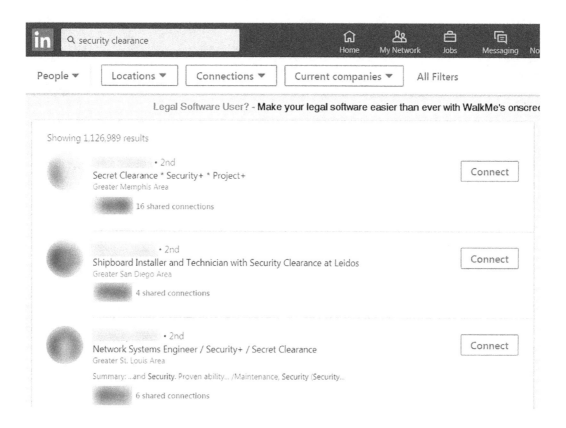

You'll see a list of people who have the keyword Security Clearance in their profile. Don't you want to appear on lists like this for your target keywords?

A strong LinkedIn presence will help you appear in Google searches as well. LinkedIn is the social network that most often appears at the top of Google search results, ranking "higher than all other profiles including all other social networks and website builders."[14] So even if you don't care about showing up in LinkedIn searches, if you want to rank on Google, make sure to optimize your keywords on LinkedIn.

Option: If you need professional assistance with crafting your headline, contact The Essay Expert.[15] All of our LinkedIn packages[16] include a custom headline that will help you move up in LinkedIn search rankings.

Mistake #2

Unprofessional/Distracting Profile Photo, No Photo, or No Background Image

The Problem

Having no LinkedIn profile photo means your profile is not 100% complete. It also leaves your audience with only words to go on, and your profile will likely be skipped in favor of those with professional photos. According to LinkedIn,[17] profiles with photos receive 21 times more views and 9x more connection requests than those without. Think about it: If you were to look at two profiles side by side, and both people had the same qualifications, and the only difference was that one person had a photo and the other did not, which one would you look at first? You might even wonder whether the person without a photo could be a spammer (there are plenty of those on LinkedIn).

Photos are particularly important for job seekers, since recruiters report they like to see photos in profiles. A study by Ladders[18] revealed that when recruiters review your profile, they spend one fifth of that time looking at your photo! If your photo includes your dog, cat, husband, or a lot of unnecessary objects in the background, viewers might think you're immature or unprofessional, or simply be distracted; and it will be hard to focus on YOU. If you are not looking at the camera, people might not be inclined to trust you as a capable business person.

Similarly, if you have a LinkedIn Premium account, having no background image leaves your profile lacking the simple magnetic power a stunning photo could add. Here's what the standard boring blue background looks like:

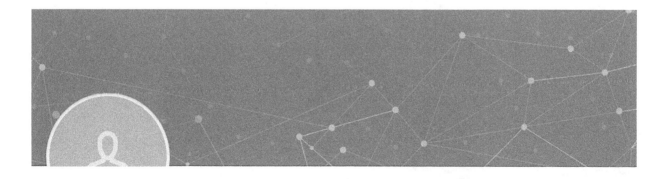

The Tune-Up

Photos

Get a professional head shot with a plain background. If possible, find someone who does "branded photography" which is a way you can ensure your personality comes through your photo. If a professional photo is not an option, stand outside on a bright day, in an open space, and get a friend to take a close-up. Use natural light (not a flash, which can create shadows). Smile and look directly at the camera. Make sure you portray yourself as you want to be seen by your intended audience.

If your photo is too small for the new image size, update it!

LinkedIn's official profile photo guidelines:
- Format should be jpg, gif or png.
- Photos should be square.
- Ideal pixel size is 400 x 400, and should not exceed 20,000 pixels.
- File size should not exceed 8MB.

Tip: For all LinkedIn images dimensions, see **Appendix C**.

Here are what I believe to be some effective profile photos on LinkedIn:

Michael Cavotta · 1st
authentic headshots + all things personal branding

Susan (Schmidt) Thomson · 1st
CEO ActionCOACH Business & Executive Coaching, Buy Build Sell WI, Board Director-WEA Trust, Neugen, HealthTraditions

Dr. Pelè — Storybound Marketing • 1st

Would You Like To Enroll Your Highest-Value Clients On LinkedIn?

Lori (Lori Coleman) Terry • 2nd

Caterer, Private Chef & Cooking Instructor

Note: Depending on your industry, you might choose to post a more or less formal photo. If you work in the music industry, perhaps you might choose a more colorful pose!

Bright, solid colors can help you stand out among a sea of other connections.

Once you have the perfect pic, view this quick video on how to enhance your profile photo using LinkedIn's editing and photo filtering tools.[19] Learn how to zoom in and crop your photo to the perfect size every time, plus add a variety of filters for a more modern look.

Background Image

LinkedIn allows all users to add a background image to your profile. To create a unique background, begin with a 1400×425 pixel jpg image that depicts your brand. Go to your profile page by clicking on your profile preview in the left column:

Or you can click on "Me" in the upper right of your menu bar and select "View profile":

Click on the pencil icon to access your editor.
In the upper right of the background image area, you'll see another pencil icon.

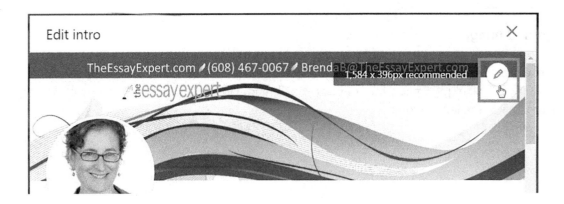

Click the pencil to access a pop-up window where you can upload your image and edit it.

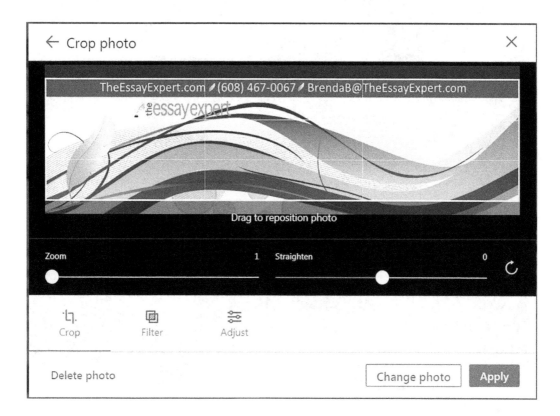

Here are what I believe to be some effective profile backgrounds on LinkedIn:

Videographer & Photographer | Graphic Artist

Personal Injury/Civil Litigation

✦ Executive Level Program Manager ✦ Problem Solver ✦ Tactical Execution ✦ Leads Technical & Security Teams to Deliver ✦

• 1st

BUSINESS PORTRAITS FOR INDIVIDUALS AND GROWING COMPANIES

What's the right image for you? You get to choose.

A Note About Privacy

You might have a concern that people could start harassing you due to your public photo. I myself have had a few people contact me under the guise of a professional connection when they seemed more interested in flirtation!

As an alternative to posting your photo publicly, you can change your photo settings to be visible only to your connections or only to your network (see **Appendix H**). This step may deter someone from asking for a connection based on visual interests alone. However, the downside is that you lose the very important advantages of having a profile photo. Also, keep in mind that your network circle consists of 1st, 2nd and 3rd tier connections and can reach farther than you think.

To set the visibility of your profile photo, go to your profile and click on your photo. Click on Visibility, then select who can see your profile: everyone on LinkedIn, just your network, or just your connections.

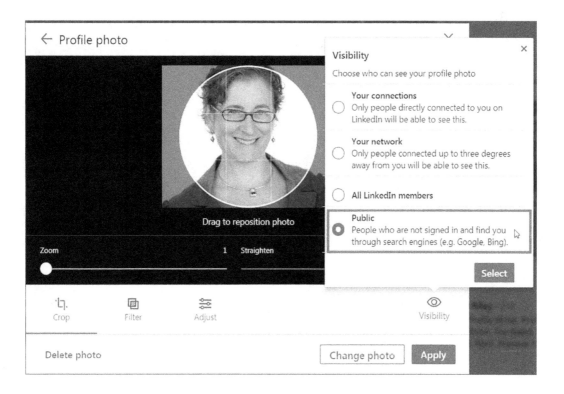

To make your photo invisible in web searches (or to anyone not logged into LinkedIn), go to your profile and click on the "Edit your public profile" link in the upper right.

This will bring you to a page where you can set the visibility for each element of your profile when someone searches for you outside of LinkedIn.

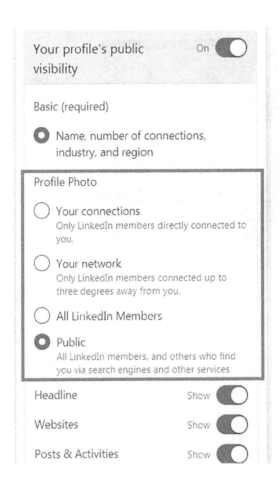

For more information on Privacy concerns, see **Mistake #5**.

A Note About Discrimination

Some people do not post a photo on LinkedIn because of concerns about age or race discrimination. Note that I can't give you legal advice. What I can say is that the reality is discrimination happens even though of course it is illegal. My question for you would be: Would you want to work for a company that doesn't contact you because of something they see in your picture? If they are going to discriminate, chances are they will do it in the interview if they don't have a chance to make judgments based on your photo. And the fact is, you will almost certainly be discriminated against for not posting a photo at all, since people are naturally more interested when they have a visual picture of the person they are contacting.

That said, if you are 50+ and concerned about age discrimination, it can't hurt to post a photo that makes you look as youthful as possible. Age is just a number, and your photo can give a sense of your energy and enthusiasm about your life and career!

Creating a Custom Background Image

There are several methods for creating a custom background image for your LinkedIn profile. Here are a few that I've discovered:

1. Canva

Canva[20] is a handy tool for creating professional-quality social media graphics, including custom banners for LinkedIn. Many of their ready-made LinkedIn banner templates[21] are free to use and are highly customizable. Add your name, logo and even embellish a bit more depending on the template you choose. Sign up is free.

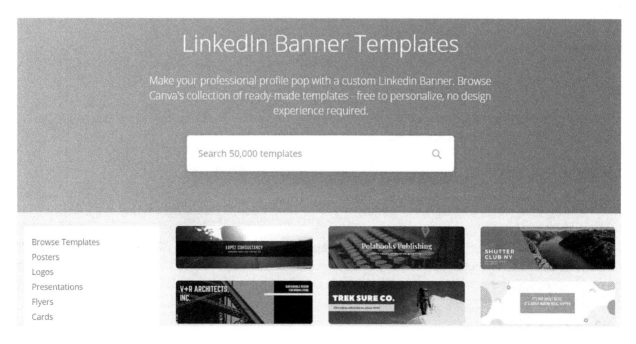

2. Fotor

Fotor[22] Photo Editor is a free online designer and editing tool and collage creator. Go to https://www.fotor.com/templates/linkedin-background to see all of the templates they have to offer. Or, create your own by clicking the "Collage" option on the home page. In the left sidebar, click "Create New Work" and select the Classic style of collage.

LinkedIn's background image dimensions are 1584 (w) x 396 (h) pixels. To change the size of the collage, click the lock icon to unlock the dimensions and Apply. From there you can create a tiled background using your own images. Here's an example:

3. Adobe Spark

Adobe Spark works much like Canva and Fotor to create a banner. Sign up for your account, then go to https://spark.adobe.com/sp/design/post/new to select your banner size.

Spark's free version does contain a watermark in the lower right corner; however, their premium is only $9.99/mo.

4. Free LinkedIn Backgrounds[23]

This site has a nice variety of photo backgrounds to choose from. You can start with one of these and use Canva or Fotor to add your logo.

There are also many free photo editing software platforms out there that will allow you to create an image, including paint.net and Pixlr Editor.[24]

Results to Expect

According to Link for Small Business, "adding a profile photo could result in 14 times more views than someone without."

An engaging profile photo and background create a personal relationship with your viewers. You will be more likely to be contacted by many recruiters. People will see you as friendly and professional and will be encouraged to read more about you. They might even be inspired to do business with you.

Mistake #3

Not Creating an All-Star Profile

The Problem

Although LinkedIn has stopped telling you exactly what comprises a "complete" or "All Star" profile, and although you're the only person who will be able to view the strength of your own profile, it's clear that if your profile is missing certain information, you will not rank as highly in LinkedIn searches. Plus, LinkedIn will keep bugging you with questions, egging you on to strengthen your profile every time you view it. This is one of the easiest items to handle, so why not take action?

There are five levels of profile strength, based on your level of completeness: Beginner, Intermediate, Advanced, Expert and All-Star. I'd like you to be an All-Star by the end of this book!

The Tune-Up

The most basic way to move your strength meter up is to fill in all the sections of your profile. The meter will increase as you add more content (for example a photo, a location, an education entry, an industry, or a position), until you will receive an All-Star profile.

You can view your profile strength meter in the upper right-hand corner of Your Dashboard, which you'll find just below your Summary.

Your Dashboard		☆ All Star
Private to you		
1,094	16	279
Who viewed your profile	Article views	Search appearances

Below your dashboard, LinkedIn will give you some advice on any sections of your profile that need improvement. Answer the questions posed by LinkedIn to strengthen your profile.

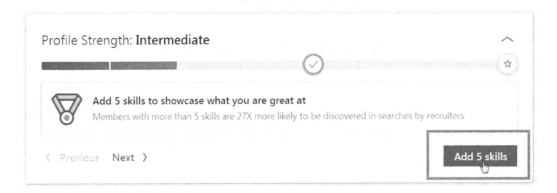

Note that if you've created a custom headline (see **Mistake #1**) and LinkedIn asks you whether one of your positions is your current title, clicking "Yes" will replace your headline with your position title. Don't do it! Similarly, if you add a new position to your Experience section, be sure to uncheck the "Update my headline" option or LinkedIn will replace your custom Headline with this position title.

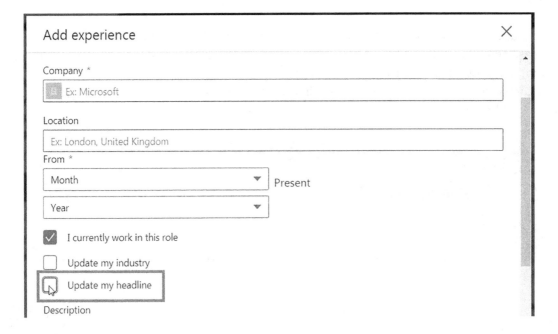

Completing the following items will give you a good start on increasing your LinkedIn strength:

- Your industry and location (More than 30% of recruiters search by location, and according to Link Humans, "adding an industry could get your 15 times more profile views." LinkedIn reports that more than 300,000 people search by industry on LinkedIn every week![25]

- An up-to-date current position (with a description)

** Note that if you've created a custom headline (see **Mistake #1**) and you add a new position to your Experience section, you must uncheck the "Update my headline" option or LinkedIn will replace your custom Headline with this position title (I believe this is how LinkedIn attempts to trick members into not crafting their own keyword-optimized headline. I don't know why they do it).

- At least two past positions. According to LinkedIn,[26] your profile gets viewed up to 29 more times if you have more than one position listed in your Experience section.

- Your education, including the details requested by LinkedIn. (According to Link Humans, "members who have an education on their profile receive an average of 10 times more profile views than those who don't" as well as 17 times more messages from recruiters.)

- Your skills (minimum of 3)

- A profile photo

- At least 50 connections

Perhaps the most controversial of these items is "current position." What should you put here if you are not employed? There is no definitive answer to this question. The fact is, if your profile is missing this item, yet you have taken all the other advice in this book, you will still have a strong profile and do quite well in searches.

If you don't have a current position, you might choose to list your job title as the position you are seeking, and your "company" as "--" or as "Open to New Opportunities." Some recruiters do search for that keyword phrase; however, some recruiters are turned off by it. See **Bonus Tip #4** for more on this topic.

The good news is that your LinkedIn profile is a living document and you can always try something one way for a month or two, then try something different for another period.

Your Contact Information

While it's not officially counted as part of an All-Star profile, I can't emphasize enough how important it is to include your contact information, including your email address and phone number, in your LinkedIn profile. I am constantly shocked at how many people do not include this information and thus make it difficult for anyone to contact them.

As an aside, I'm also shocked at how many people do not look up my contact information simply by clicking on the "See contact info" link, and who request my email address by IM when they could easily obtain it from my profile. If you're asking people for information you could find easily yourself, you're not truly a LinkedIn superuser—you might, however, be a user.

Brenda Bernstein
Resume & LinkedIn Profile Writer, Author, Speaker ★
Executive Resumes ★ C-Level Resumes ★ Executive LinkedIn
Profiles ★ College Essays ★ Law School Admissions Essays ★
MBA Admissions Essays

New Haven, Connecticut

The Essay Expert LLC

New York University School of Law

See contact info

See connections (500+)

Click and you shall receive!

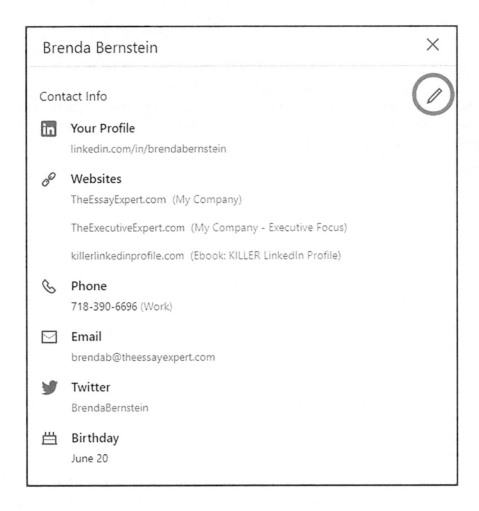

It's easy to edit your contact information on LinkedIn. Simply click on "See contact info" in your own introduction card, which will bring you to a window where you can click on the pencil (edit) icon:

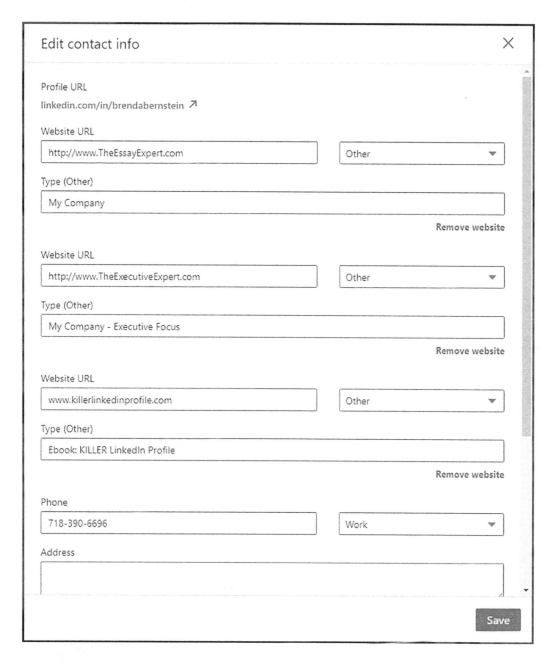

Should I include my personal details?

If you're comfortable receiving phone calls from LinkedIn connections, include a phone number. If not, don't. But be aware that you could be skipped over if you don't include it.

I have my phone number listed and have rarely gotten any inappropriate calls. That said, I would recommend posting non-personal numbers here that only ring during business hours.

I would also recommend creating a separate e-mail account for your LinkedIn emails. When you accept a connection request, that person can obtain your email address and put you on a list without your permission. So be aware that you could be opening yourself up for spam by including an email address in the Contact Info section. I think it's worth the hassle, but the ultimate decision is up to you.

Birthdays? I'd say they're not that important, and there's definitely no need to include a year. If you want happy birthday messages on LinkedIn to add to the mess of good wishes on Facebook, go for it! Otherwise, not.

Finally, as former recruiter Catherine Byers Breet emphasizes, you will get mileage out of including your contact information in your LinkedIn Summary section. Recruiters are in a hurry, so the easier you make it for them to contact you, the better! (If you are worried about privacy, create a free email address that you use just for LinkedIn contacts, and/or a free phone number through a provider such as GoogleVoice.)

See **Bonus Tip #2** to learn how to make sure your contact information is easily accessed by the people who want to reach out to you.

Results to Expect

Completing your profile is one of the easiest paths to a KILLER LinkedIn Profile.

With a strong profile, you will rank more highly in searches, and, according to LinkedIn, your profile will be 40 times more likely to be viewed. Your profile ranking will increase, perhaps as high as to All-Star, which will appear when you view your own profile.

The chart in the Introduction section of this book bears repeating and shows clearly that the more comprehensive your LinkedIn profile, the more likely you are to be contacted by recruiters:

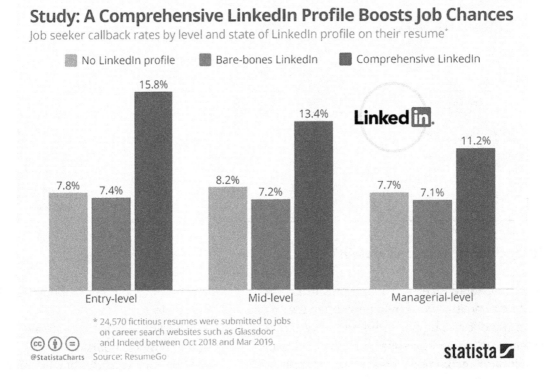

Study: A Comprehensive LinkedIn Profile Boosts Job Chances

Job seeker callback rates by level and state of LinkedIn profile on their resume*

* 24,570 fictitious resumes were submitted to jobs on career search websites such as Glassdoor and Indeed between Oct 2018 and Mar 2019.

@StatistaCharts   Source: ResumeGo

statista

Note that a comprehensive LinkedIn profile can give you from a 4.1% to a 8.4% better chance of a callback over a bare-bones one.

Not only that, but the more complete your profile is, the more likely you are to rank highly in Google searches (be sure to have your profile "Public" so that people can Google you).

Including your contact information means that the people who want to connect with you will be more likely to reach out.

Have fun going for the stars!

Your Dashboard
Private to you

☆ All Star

1,094	16	279
Who viewed your profile	Article views	Search appearances

Mistake #4

Outdated or Incomplete Information in Contact and Personal Info

The Problem

In your Contact and Personal Info section, found on the right side of your introduction card, visitors can view your LinkedIn URL and up to three websites of your choice, plus your phone number, email, Twitter handle, and birthday. If you fill in your birthday, be prepared to get happy birthday messages galore on LinkedIn. If you don't complete your contact information, well, people might not be able to reach you privately if they want to. And since this is a networking site, don't you want to make it easy for people to find you?

Your Public Profile URL is the first thing people see in this section. It's the link that brings people to your LinkedIn profile page.

LinkedIn creates a Public Profile URL for you that contains lots of slashes and numbers at the end. All this gobbledygook (to use a technical term) prevents brand recognition. If you leave your Public URL as LinkedIn's default, your readers will be left with letters and numbers instead of your name. "http://www.linkedin.com/in/brendabernstein/13/72a/a64" just isn't as memorable as "https://www.linkedin.com/in/brendabernstein/" It takes up a lot more room on your resume or business card too.

The websites section of LinkedIn is even more important than you might think. Google ranks web addresses on LinkedIn very highly, so if you don't list your company website(s) on LinkedIn, you're squandering a valuable SEO opportunity.

The Tune-Up

Profile URL

First, let's talk about customizing your LinkedIn URL. You can change your URL to a "vanity" URL that ends with your name by clicking on "Edit public profile & URL" in the right sidebar of your profile.

Then click on your Profile URL and you will land here:

At the top of the right-hand column you will see "Edit public profile URL." Click on the pencil icon to reveal an entry field where you can customize away!

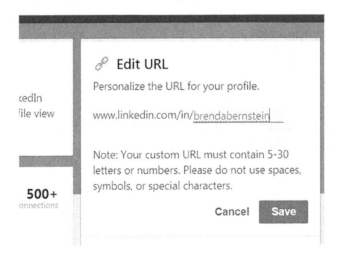

Is the name you want unavailable? Try your last name followed by your first name; or use a credential or keyword. Find a solution that works for you! Keep in mind that the custom ending to your URL must be between 5 and 29 characters and may not include any spaces or "special characters" which include dashes, dots and other symbols.

Important Note: If you have your original Public Profile URL on your resume, business card, e-mail signature or any other materials, that old URL will redirect to your new URL. However, if you change the customized URL to a different customized URL, the first customized URL will not redirect to the second one!

**Keyword Tip: If you have room to add keywords at the end of your profile URL, you can get search engine optimization (SEO) mileage out of adding your top keyword directly after your name! For instance, johnjonescorporatecounsel or janesmithitdirector. Adding these keywords will not affect your search rankings within LinkedIn itself, but it will provide some leverage in Google searches.

**Resume Tip: I credit this tip to a client who told me he had purchased his name.com domain and then pointed the domain to his LinkedIn page. If you don't already own yourname.com for other purposes, such as a blog or other job search marketing materials, this option might be a good one for you. For example, instead of listing your profile at the top of your resume as "https://www.linkedin.com/in/brendabernstein," you could write "LinkedIn profile: www.brendabernstein.com," which looks much cleaner and also shows that you are tech-savvy.

Website URLs

Speaking of websites, have you listed yours in the Contact and Personal Info section? See **Mistake #3** for information on how to edit your contact information. You'll click on the pencil icon in the Contact Info section:

Here's what the screen looks like where you can edit your website info:

Type in your information and select the type of link you are adding. Then from the drop-down, select the appropriate choice. If you don't like the choices, no problem—just say "Other" and you'll be able to enter anything you want in the "Type (Other)" box that appears.

If your company has a special landing page you want LinkedIn users to see, feel free to list that page as one of the three websites.

Another great option for sharing websites is to post them in your Publications or even your Projects section. See **Mistake #14** for more information on the ever-important Special Sections.

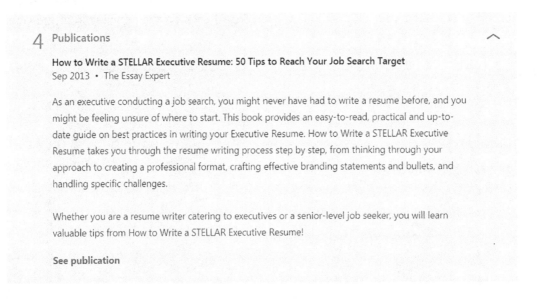

Results to Expect

With a customized LinkedIn URL, your name will stand out and provide a cleaner image on your resume, business cards, or anywhere else you are sharing your LinkedIn URL. Your Google search rankings will improve based on the inclusion of your name as well as keywords if space allows.

Updating your websites and other contact information will give your viewers more ability to find out who you are, and to contact you if they want to. The easier it is for people to discover and reach you, the more results you'll get from LinkedIn.

Finally, if you work for or own a company, putting a link to your company's website on LinkedIn will boost the company's Google page rank. Here's how The Essay Expert shows up with a Google search for "theessayexpert.com":

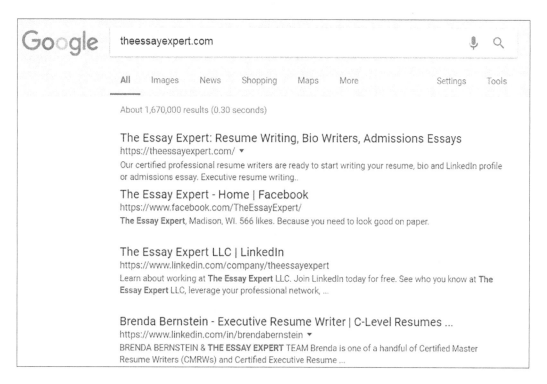

As you can see, LinkedIn shows up as the third and fourth results on the page. That's the kind of SEO you want for your company.

Mistake #5

Fewer than 500 (or even 1,000) Connections

The number of Connections you have appears to the right of your location:

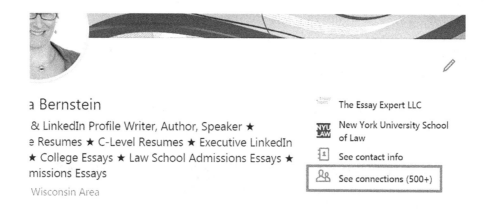

ə Bernstein

& LinkedIn Profile Writer, Author, Speaker ★
ə Resumes ★ C-Level Resumes ★ Executive LinkedIn
★ College Essays ★ Law School Admissions Essays ★
missions Essays

Wisconsin Area

The Essay Expert LLC

New York University School of Law

See contact info

See connections (500+)

The Problem

Statista.com[27] reported that as of March 2016, 27% of LinkedIn users had between 500 and 999 first degree connections on the site, with another 28% having more than that. I'm willing to bet these numbers have skyrocketed since then.

Depending on your intention with your profile, you might be putting yourself at a big disadvantage by having fewer than 500 connections—and I would assert that you really need more than 1,000. With a smaller network, your updates will go to a limited audience; the people who view your profile might see you as "unconnected"; and, perhaps most important, you will often not appear in searches if you are not connected on at least a 2nd degree level to the people conducting the search.

In fact, someone could search for you by your actual name and not find you if you do not have at least a 2nd degree connection to that person! So it is absolutely critical that you increase your number of connections.

There are admittedly some advantages to having fewer connections, or at least to having carefully-chosen connections, as outlined in the article, "Looking for a Job? Having Too Many Contacts on LinkedIn May Backfire."[28] This report, based on a limited study by The University of Texas at Austin, points out that if you want to increase your ability to obtain referrals, as opposed to just job leads, you must have a strong network of people who know you well. I would suggest that a large network and a strong network are not mutually exclusive, and that every power LinkedIn user would benefit from building both.

Another reason to expand your network is that LinkedIn has made it more and more difficult to communicate with people who are not your 1st degree connections. You've probably experienced searching for someone and having results come up that suggest you must send InMail or subscribe to LinkedIn®

Premium in order to write to the person you're trying to reach. Perhaps even the person's last name is unavailable to you. And the Connect button is nowhere to be found! This is certainly a bind you want to get out of.

The Tune-Up

There is a balance to be struck between expanding your network as aggressively as possible and expanding it with quality connections. Your strategy will be different depending on your situation. If you are a CEO or Corporate Counsel or a VP of Asset Management at a Hedge Fund, you will make different choices than if you are an internet marketer or a resume writer. Choose your connections based on the image you want to project as well as your goal with your LinkedIn profile.

As a general rule, the more people you are connected with within your field or client base, the more leverage you will get from your connections. Additionally, the more connections your connections have, the more rapidly your network will expand.

One easy way to expand your network is to accept connection requests from people you know or whom you would want to know. You will get connection requests directly by email, or you can view them by going to the upper right-hand corner of your LinkedIn page and clicking on "My Network":

On the resulting page, you will have the opportunity to accept or ignore the connection requests you've received.

If you see the words "See more" in the invitation, that means the person has taken the good advice of many LinkedIn experts and sent you a personal message along with their request. Click on the "See more" link to view the message and then click on the blue "Reply to [connection's name]" below the message to respond.

By writing a message in response to invitations, and not just accepting them, you can make a more personal connection that spurs dialog and may even lead to new job and business opportunities. My favorite response from a LinkedIn connection read, "Thank you, thank you! Tonight I'm going to read your book to my kids. It's never too early to start building your LinkedIn network."

Whenever someone reaches out to connect with me, I give them a few tips on their profile. This practice has built trust with my network and even attracted some clients. Likewise, when people have offered me advice after connecting with me, I've been spurred to speak with and even hire some of them!

Some professionals have a rule that they will only connect with someone after a phone call or in-person conversation. This practice is a great way to meet people in an authentic way and to create valuable alliances.

Following are some suggestions of ways to reach out yourself to expand your network responsibly. Choose the options that work best for you!

LinkedIn Search

If you know the name of the person you want to connect with, simply type that name into the search bar. Let's say you're looking for Jane Smith. You'll get a list which you can then narrow by People, Jobs, Posts, Companies, Groups or Schools. Note, however, that if the person does not have 500+ connections, it's possible that you can type in their name and they will not show up in your search.

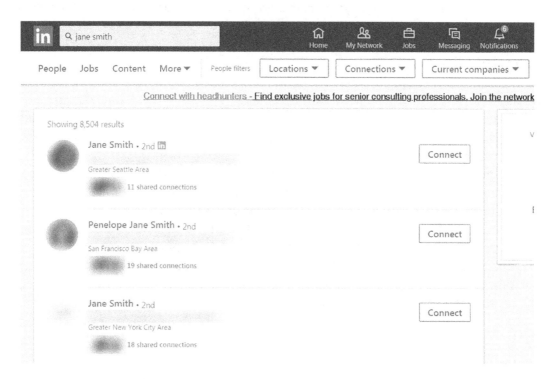

If you type "jane smith photographer" you'll get a different results list:

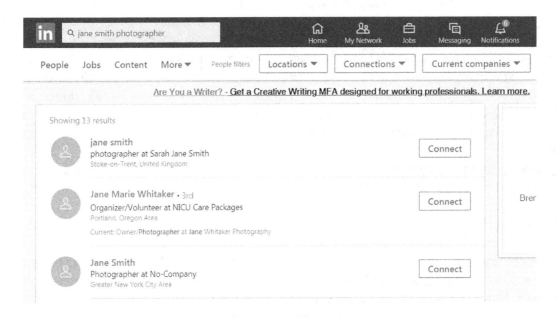

Boolean logic is available to refine your search. For more details on how to use this method, read LinkedIn Help's article, Using Boolean Search on LinkedIn.[29]

Your Address Book

One easy way to build your LinkedIn network is by sending requests to people in your address book. If they are already LinkedIn members, they will accept your invitation almost 100% of the time. If they are not members, many will join LinkedIn at your request, because they trust you and they've probably been thinking about joining for a long time anyway.

Before I share how to get a list of your contacts, let me say that I do NOT recommend having LinkedIn invite everyone in your address book to become members! Many of them might be outdated, and they could reject your invitation, creating some issues for you with the LinkedIn powers that be. However, you can use this feature to get a list of people you might want to invite personally.

In essence, you'll proceed **as if** you're going to add your contacts, but you won't do it. Here's how:

Click on the "My Network" tab. In the left sidebar under "Your Connections" and click "Continue." If you're not already logged into your email account, and you have a web-hosted mail like Gmail, Yahoo, Comcast, etc., enter the email address you'd like LinkedIn to access and click "Continue":

Once logged in, you'll be taken to a screen similar to this (it will vary depending on your email program) where you can grant LinkedIn permission to access your email:

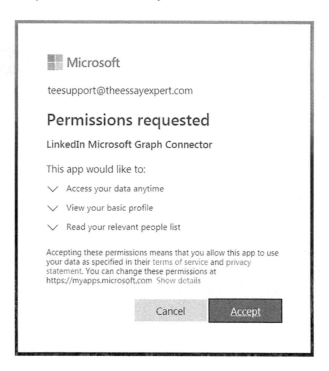

Click "Accept" and you will get a list of people in your e-mail address book who are current members of LinkedIn.

Connect with people you know on LinkedIn

We found 1,247 people you know on LinkedIn. Select the people you'd like to connect to.   Step 1 of 2

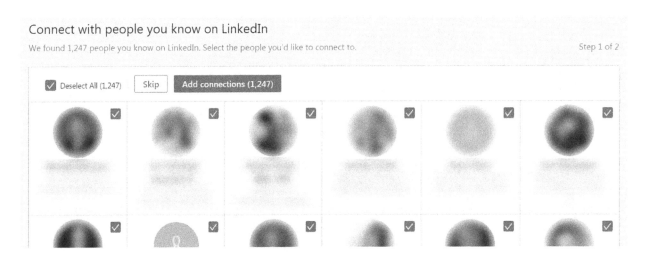

This is so important I am going to say it again!! I do NOT recommend sending invitations to your contacts using this feature! They will receive an invitation with no message, you will risk getting an unacceptable number of rejections, and LinkedIn will temporarily limit you from requesting more connections. If this happens, you'll need to manually withdraw as many invitations as possible.

To do this, go to your My Network tab and click on "Manage all," then view your sent connection requests.

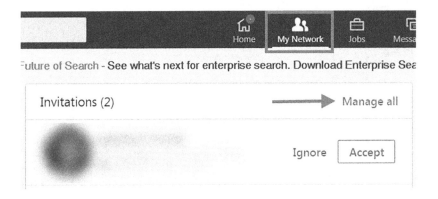

To avoid this unnecessary hassle, instead look at the list and note the people with whom you would like to connect. Then visit each profile, click "Connect," and send them a personal message. Since they are in your address book, you most definitely have their e-mail address, which you may need to provide.

Alumni

I recommend connecting with alumni from your educational institutions. To find alumni, put the name of your school in the main search bar and then click on your school from the drop-down.

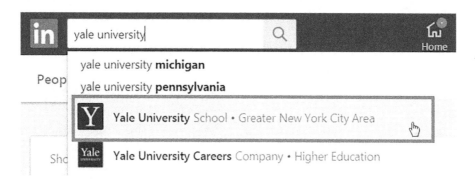

You'll be taken to a page where you can then click on "See alumni."

With this feature, you will have the opportunity to send invitations with personalized messages to each of your desired connections. You can invite a new connection to your network, or find those who are already 1st level connections. Use the "Next" button to find the "How you are connected" column and click on "1st Connections."

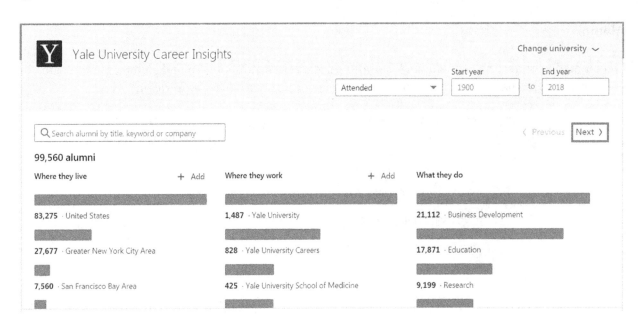

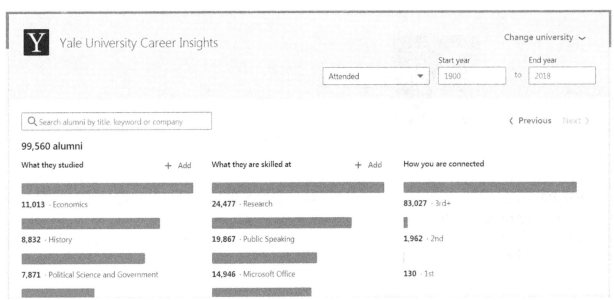

Scroll down to find alumni you can connect with. Then click on "Connect" to send a message.

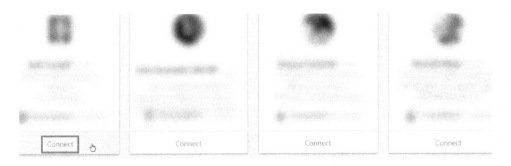

For more information on connecting with alumni, go to The Best Way to Network with Alumni on LinkedIn.[30] The feature is quite robust, allowing you to sort alumni by date, location, company, career, field of study, skills and connection level. Don't miss out on this opportunity to start up conversations with your fellow classmates; you have an automatic connection with them and they are likely to want to help you!

[Word of warning, especially for older job seekers: If you search for alumni by date and the person has not entered their dates of school attendance, you will not find them by searching with a date range. Similarly, if you do not enter your dates of education, you will not be found by your classmates if they search by date. You need to consider the benefits of hiding your age vs. the benefits of connecting with alumni from your class.]

> **Important!** If you want to be found as an alumnus or alumna of an educational institution, you must enter a school that LinkedIn recognizes. Here's what to keep in mind:
>
> When adding a school to your Education section, you want the logo of the school to appear if possible, since that is what will link the school to the Alumni feature on LinkedIn. The first field to complete will be the school name. Begin typing the name to reveal a listing.

Select the correct school and once you have saved your entry, the school's logo will appear on your profile.

If the entity you want doesn't appear in the drop-down list when you begin typing the name into that field, you may have some luck searching for the school on the web and seeing if they have a link to their LinkedIn page. Sometimes the LinkedIn icon will even show up in the Google results themselves. Here's an example from the University of Oxford:

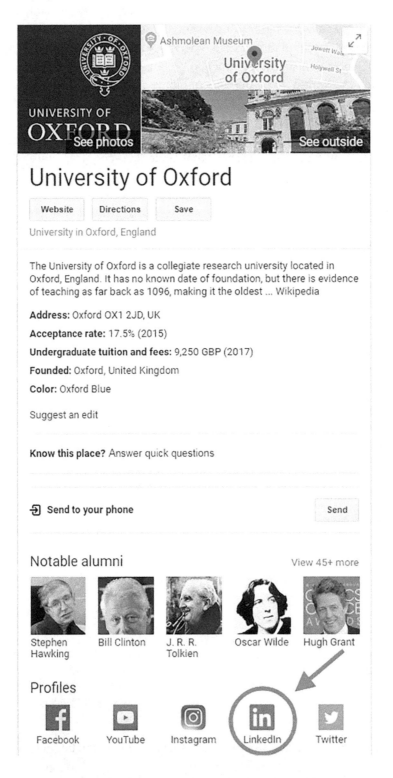

Click on the LinkedIn icon and you'll go straight to Oxford's LinkedIn page, which will make it easy to connect the school to your Education section (if you actually went there of course!).

The same goes for "alumni" of past companies.

If you want to be found as a past employee of a company, make sure you enter a company name in your Experience section that LinkedIn recognizes. The surest way to do that is to use the name that generates a logo automatically on LinkedIn.

Group Members

Another potential source of connections are your LinkedIn groups. If someone posts an interesting conversation or comment, compliment the person in your request to connect. The people in your LinkedIn groups are likely to be interested in connecting with people like you. And you can message them without needing to be officially connected first! Note that LinkedIn limits the number of 1:1 group member messages you can send to 15 per month. Read more about communicating with a fellow group member at https://www.linkedin.com/help/linkedin/answer/192?lang=en.

Troubleshooting Connection Challenges

The first challenge you might run into is in conducting a search. If you have a free membership and you perform a lot of searches, you might run into this when you're looking for people on LinkedIn:

Brenda, you're approaching the commercial use limit.

Please upgrade to LinkedIn Premium Business, Sales Navigator, or Recruiter to get unlimited people browsing.

Upgrade for Free   Learn more

You can learn more about LinkedIn's Commercial Use Limit on their website.[31] Thankfully, there are two workarounds for this issue!

1. **TOP SECRET SEARCH TIP!** Let's say you're looking for a photographer and LinkedIn tells you you've reached your limit. Try going to https://www.linkedin.com/title/photographer and see if you get the results you want. [Looking for something else? Change the word "photographer" to whatever profession you're seeking.] Multiple words should behyphenated.

2. **GOOGLE!** Google is a secret weapon for any LinkedIn search. If LinkedIn won't let you search for Jane Smith in Atlanta, search on Google for "Jane Smith Atlanta LinkedIn" and you might find her. This trick works better for people with unusual names.

Assuming you make it to someone's profile and click to connect with them, you may very well run into your next obstacle: a page like this, where your only option is to provide the connection's email address:

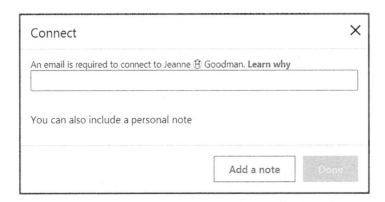

According to the LinkedIn® Help Center,[32] an email address is needed for an invitation when:

- The recipient's email preferences are set to only receive invitations from members who know their email address.

- A number of recipients have clicked "I don't know this person" after getting your invitations. (To limit the number of people who claim they don't know you, send a personal note to remind them who you are and explain why you want to connect).

When you want to connect with someone and don't have the person's email address, try the following:

1. Look in the person's LinkedIn profile. You might find an email address somewhere if you look carefully!

2. Search for the person's name and title on Google. They may have a bio page listed with a contact email.

3. Look up the person's company on Google and see how the company addresses are created. If you see other people with addresses like SamA@ABC.com or PaulaD@ABC.com, you can be pretty sure of the address for your targeted contact.

Important: Do NOT enter a random email address and think you have beat the system! If you do not enter an email address that matches an address associated with the LinkedIn member, your request will not be sent and you will not be notified.

What if someone doesn't have your address and wants to connect with you?

Remember that other people are trying to connect with you too! Make it easy for them by setting your privacy settings so people don't need your address to connect with you (see **Appendix H** for how).

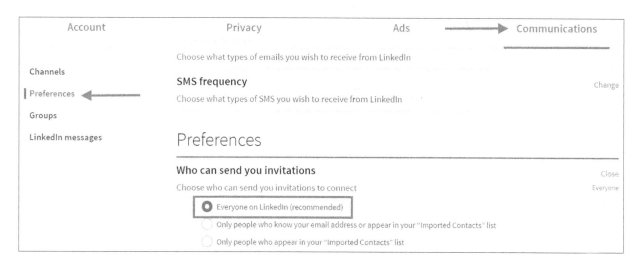

If you decide to require people to list your email address, put as many of your email addresses in the LinkedIn system as possible. Some of your connections might have an old email address or one you do not use very often. Listing multiple email addresses in your contact information will increase the possibility that your past contacts will be able to connect.

To enter additional email addresses for your account, go to your Account tab. Under "Login and security," click on "Email addresses":

Scroll down and click on "Add email address." You will then need to verify the address. Adding as many email addresses as possible will make it easy for people to contact you, no matter where they know you from.

Requesting an Introduction

If you feel comfortable, you can ask someone else to introduce you to a LinkedIn member, using the "Mutual Connections" link. Note that this feature is only available using the mobile app. Here's how:

Find a member you'd like to meet, scroll down to the Contact section, and copy their profile URL. Then scroll back up to the Highlights section. There you'll see how many mutual connections you share.

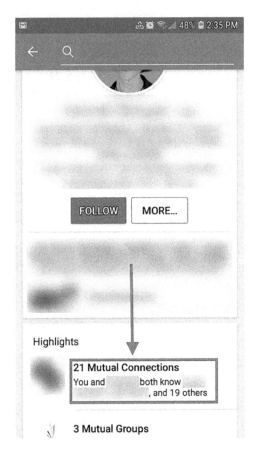

Clicking the link will take you to a list of your mutual connections.

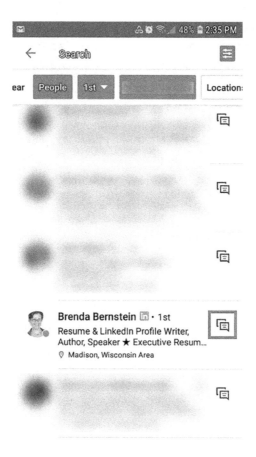

Click on the messaging icon next to the person's name who can introduce you and send a message with your request! Paste in the contact's profile URL, so your introducer knows who you want to be introduced to.

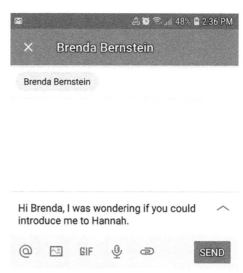

Requesting an introduction may seem intimidating, but if your 1st degree contact knows both you and the person you would like to meet, they will likely be happy to make the connection. However, it's also possible that they don't know them, in which case, your request may be denied. Don't give up! You can try the other 1st degree contacts from your "Mutual Connections" list. Remember, the more connections you have, the easier it will be to connect with almost anyone on LinkedIn.

"No InMail Credits"?

You might not be able to connect with some Premium users if they have set their privacy settings to require InMail. There might not be a way around that unless you connect with them outside of LinkedIn and ask them to send you an invitation.

Even in this situation, if you receive an invitation from someone with a Premium account, after you accept it you might see this message:

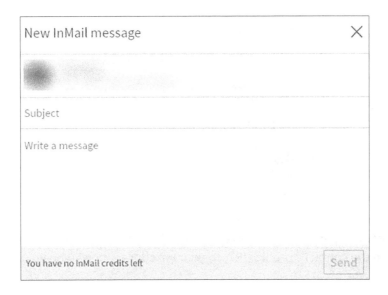

I believe LinkedIn does this to persuade you to purchase a paid membership. However, if you simply click on the person's name in the left-hand column, you'll be able to send a message:

Similarly, if you try to connect with someone and it looks like your only option is "Send InMail," that might not really be the case. Try clicking on the button with three dots below the person's headline to see the menu, which will likely give you an option to connect.

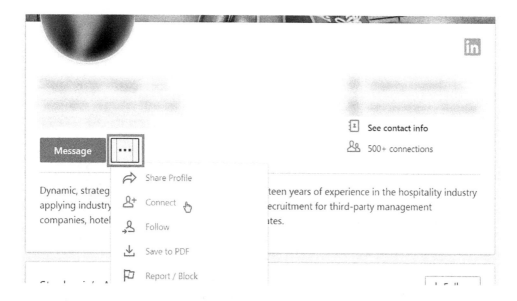

Who's viewed my profile?

A great source of connections—including, if you are doing business development or sales on LinkedIn, potential customers—can be the people who visit your profile. But who are they?

For valuable information on your visitors, go to your homepage and look below your Summary to see how many people have viewed your profile in the past 90 days and the number of times your profile appeared in search results in the last week.

If you click on the box with the number of people who have viewed your profile, you will be brought to a screen with a list of your most recent visitors and a graph of how often people viewed you over the past 90 days.

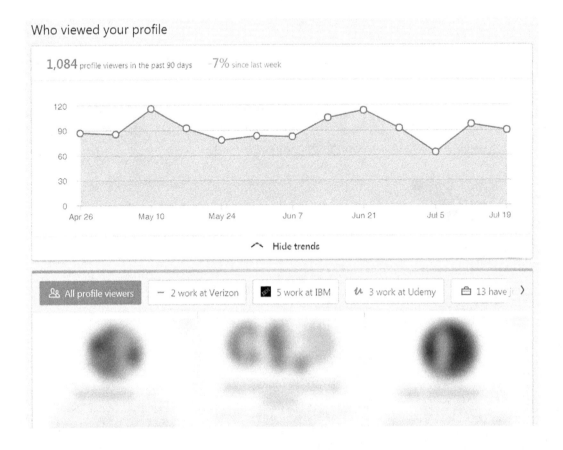

76% of LinkedIn members[33] said the "Who's Viewed Your Profile" feature was one of the most helpful tools on LinkedIn (paying members get much more value from this feature). If you are a job seeker, knowing which employers or recruiters have been visiting your profile can guide you to follow up with those individuals. You might say something like, "I noticed you viewed my profile. I am very interested in x and would like to have a conversation with you this week or next. Might we set up time to meet?"

Unfortunately, information on your viewers is extremely limited without a LinkedIn Premium membership. But you can get some details. For example, try clicking on "Weekly search appearances" from your profile page:

Your Dashboard *Private to you*		☆ All Star
1,084 Who viewed your profile	**134** Article views	**436** Search appearances

Then you'll see all this:

Weekly search stats

436

number of times your profile appeared in search results between July 10 - July 17

Where your searchers work

Forbes Coaches Council
Civic & Social Organization
11-50 employees

Society for Editors and Proofreaders (SfEP)
Nonprofit Organization Management
2-10 employees

What your searchers do

Salesperson | 7%

Business Strategist | 4%

Student | 4%

Executive Director | 4%

Founder | 3%

Keywords your searchers used

Writer

Science

Writer + Law Specialist

Law Specialist

C-Level + Writer

⑦ Want to improve future search appearances?

Have you wanted to know what search terms other members use to find your profile? Or did you think you needed a Premium subscription to be privy to that information? Here's some good news: at the bottom of your Search Appearance page, you'll see a section called "Keywords your searchers used."

This list shows the top keywords members were searching when they found and clicked on your profile in the past week. Keep in mind that most of the people who viewed your profile may not have been looking for your particular expertise, but LinkedIn's algorithm landed you into their search results.

Also look in the "What your searchers do" section to find out the most common professions of people viewing your profile.

If you're not happy with the breakdown you see, it might be time to adjust your keywords!

Want more information about who's viewed your profile?

With a free LinkedIn account, you're limited in how many people per day you can see who have viewed your profile; plus, again, if you want to know details, you will get a result that says something like, "3 LinkedIn Members."

Unlock the rest of the list with Premium

See who's interested in you with this job title plus the full list of people who viewed you in the last 90 days.

Upgrade for Free

For more detailed information about your viewers, as well as the ability to sort them in various ways and discover exactly how they found you, you must upgrade to LinkedIn® Premium (LinkedIn® Corporation will encourage you in multiple ways to do so).

Be forewarned that due to limitations members put on their profiles with their privacy settings, you might still run into roadblocks in trying to find out who has been visiting your profile; but you might get some information you would not otherwise be able to access.

Once you know who has been "checking you out," you might want to reach out. Is it a recruiter? You might be able to find out what interested them in your profile and why they didn't message you. Is it a potential client? Ditto.

Do choose carefully whether you want the people who viewed your profile to be part of your network. You don't want to connect with people who might end up spamming you.

What if I want to remove a connection?

If you add someone to your network and start to question the wisdom of that connection (e.g., the person starts spamming you with advertisements or, shall we say, "love notes"), LinkedIn makes it easy to report a message as spam. Just click the three dots in the upper right corner of your inbox message to open a "Message action" menu:

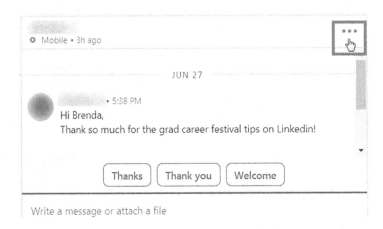

Then select "Report this conversation" and follow the prompts detailing why you want to report that person:

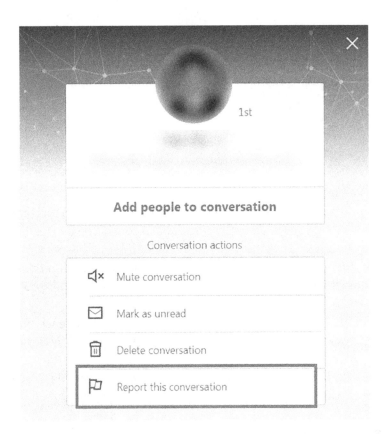

It's also easy to remove someone as a connection: Click on their name to be taken to their profile, then hover over the arrow next to the Send a message button. From the drop-down menu, select "Remove connection":

Alternatively, if the connection is very recent, you can click on My Network.

From the left sidebar, click on your number of connections:

Click the three dots to the right of the Message button and "Remove connection":

Before You Find Yourself Needing to Remove a Connection . . .

If you want to make sure the person you're about to connect to is legit, you might like to try some of the following detective-style methods recommended by my colleague, Rabbi R. Karpov, Ph.D:

Before Linking, Perform Due Diligence

First, check out the photo (we learned this "Google Images" algorithm methodology from Robin Schlinger, several years ago).

1. Click on any profile image. This opens the image in your browser. Then copy the image location/ address. If you're using Chrome as your browser, you can select "Search Google for image" and skip step 2 below. In IE, choose"Copy."

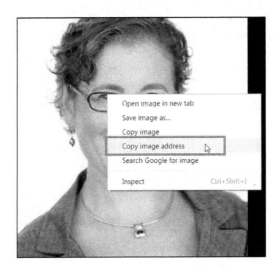

2. Next, run that photo through Google Images.[34] You can also find it by typing "google images" into your browser. Click the camera icon and paste in the image URL.

Now you can find some things out. Look for red flags:

   a. Stock photo. That wholesome-looking woman, it turns out, wasn't really an Apple Computer VP . . . nor was that her profile!

   b. Or worse: The photo is real, but it was stolen, either from someone living, such as a military-man or Miss World Philippines contestant, or from someone deceased (hey, that's *the late President of Zaire!*)

Next, check out the rest of the general "picture":

1. Run the email address you find under the connection's Contact Info through Google. Did it come up as a known email address associated ONLY with a scammer/spammer?

2. Run the connection's name through Google. What turned up?

3. Run the name AND the email address through Google. Sometimes that is what turns up information that will make you glad you took this extra 5 minutes.

A Note about Privacy Concerns

Once you connect with anyone on LinkedIn, your new connection has access to viewing people you know (if your settings are set the same way as 63% of LinkedIn users); reading every activity update you post; and sending items to your inbox. In rare instances, you may discover that you accepted an invitation you wish you hadn't. Or, you might want to block a user from seeing your profile and updates for some other reason.

Blocking a member allows you to completely remove your profile from that connection's view, and theirs from yours. In addition, says LinkedIn:

- You won't be able to message each other on LinkedIn

- If you're connected, you won't be connected anymore

- We'll remove any endorsements and recommendations from that member

- You won't see each other in your "Who's Viewed Your Profile"

- We'll stop suggesting you to each other in features such as "People You May Know"[35] and "People also Viewed"[36]

To block someone, visit their profile and click on the "More" button below the person's headline (or on the three dots to the right of their profile picture). From the drop-down menu, select "Report / Block" and you'll be able to choose to block this person, report them, report the image, or report that their account may have been hacked.

If you choose to report them, you will need to provide a reason for doing so.

Blocking a contact will automatically disconnect you. When blocking, you do not need to provide a reason:

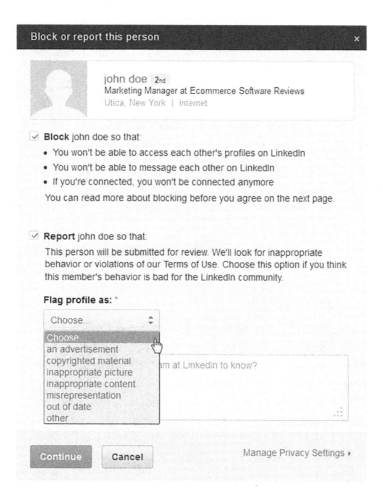

To unblock someone, click on the Privacy tab, then select "Blocking and hiding" from the left sidebar menu. To the right of the "Blocking," click "Change." From here you can unblock members, should you choose to do so.

Account	Privacy	Ads
How others see your profile and network information	**Saving job application answers** Choose if you'd like for LinkedIn to save the information you enter into job applications.	
How others see your LinkedIn activity		
How LinkedIn uses your data	## Blocking and hiding	
Job seeking preferences	**Followers**	
Blocking and hiding	Choose who can follow you and see your public updates	
	Blocking See your list, and make changes if you'd like	

Once you have blocked someone, their name will appear on your block list. You can view the list by visiting your Settings & Privacy management area.

For more information on how the blocking feature works, including how to block from within a group environment, read "Blocking or Unblocking a Member."[37]

Of course, ideally we would never want to have to block anyone, so here are a few things you can do to protect your privacy in the first place:

1. Only accept connections from people you know. LinkedIn is a great supporter of this philosophy; however, there is a trade-off between maintaining a small number of reputable connections and broadening your network (and thus increasing your leads) by connecting with people outside of your circle.

2. Change your settings under Settings & Privacy so that only those who know your email address or are in your imported contacts list can send you invitations (Go to Settings & Privacy, Communications tab, and "Select who can send you invitations"). (For more details on how to find the Settings & Privacy section, see **Appendix H.**)

3. To protect the privacy of your connections, go to Settings & Privacy, Privacy tab, and click on "How others see your profile and network information" from the left sidebar menu. Then click on "Who can see your connections" and you will have an option to prevent others from seeing see your network. This will prevent your 1st degree connections from seeing exactly how many connections you have; otherwise they will be able to get past the "500+" and see both your exact number of connections and who those connections are.

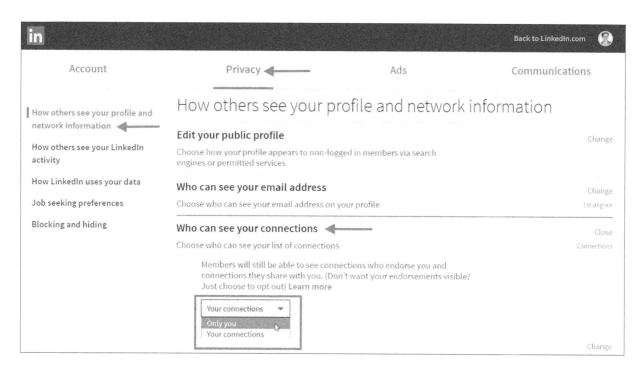

None of these alternative actions is a perfect solution. If you encounter unwanted attention on LinkedIn, it is your prerogative to block them. You may also want to report any harassment to LinkedIn® Corporation; and if necessary, please seek legal counsel.

Results to Expect

By increasing your number of connections (preferably to 1,000+), you will be much more likely to appear at the top of searches. You will also appear more frequently in "people similar to X" when potential customers or recruiters search for people similar to others that interest them. You will have more views of your page each day and each week. More people will request to connect with you because of whom you know. And you'll eventually be able to impress your viewers with that coveted "500+" connections listing on your profile!

How do you know how much activity is occurring in your account? First of all, you'll get regular emails telling you how many people are visiting your profile:

If that "1456" looks like a big number to you, keep working to increase the number in your big blue circle! Here are some of the results readers produced by implementing the suggestions in this book:

> "My WHO'S VIEWED MY PROFILE is up 324% in just a week."
> — Joe N, Graphic Designer, San Francisco, CA

> "Since incorporating many of the suggestions in your book, my average daily views have more than doubled!"
> — David Goren, National Account Manager, Atlanta, GA

> "My profile views went from 2-3 a week to 197!"
> — rquiles, Amazon Reviewer

If you are a job seeker, according to Greig Wells of BefoundJobs.com, you will get one job offer for every 300 views to your account. That means if you get 10 views a day you will likely receive a job offer within one month!!

Mistake #6

Ineffective or Inappropriate Communication with Your Network

The Problem

Once someone accepts your connection request, you have a golden opportunity to communicate with that person. Consider this a privilege not to be taken for granted. It's easy to connect with someone and then forget about them, in which case you will not get value from the connection. The other possibility is that you can communicate inappropriately and be seen as a spammer. This chapter will help you to get the most value out of your LinkedIn communications.

The Tune-Up

We're connected. Now what?

Once you're connected with someone, the most important thing is to communicate with them—and not succumb to apathy, lethargy, entropy, or any of those addictive downers. And you must communicate in a way that inspires people to respond.

What should you say in your LinkedIn messages?

Whenever you're communicating on social media, it's paramount to avoid sounding like a spammer. To that end, I do not recommend sending emails to all your connections stating that you are a job seeker and asking them if they know of any openings, or that you have the best new app since Pokémon. This type of email will be quickly forgotten at best, and result in a spam report at worst.

Job seekers:

You might want to ask your new connection, very respectfully, for advice on steps to take to have the most effective job search. If they engage with you, perhaps you can escalate to asking them whom you might approach to further your search. Do not, under any circumstances, have your first communication to a stranger be to ask them if they know of any jobs. I promise you, you will not get a positive response.

If you connect with someone at a company where you would like to work, and if they respond favorably to an initial message, try offering to take them for coffee or lunch and let them know you're interested in finding out more about what it's like to work for their organization. Again, at no point is it appropriate to ask for a job, unless this is a connection you already know well. If they like you and see an opportunity for you, they will raise that possibility. You need to have a very high level of rapport to ask directly about job opportunities at an organization. If you already know about a job there, you could ask for advice on how to best position yourself to apply for the job.

Business owners:

Do **not** send out unsolicited requests for business to your contacts. Instead, thank them for their connection, and perhaps send them an article you think they will like, comment on something you were impressed by in their profile, ask them a great question about their business, or even mention someone in your network with whom they might want to connect. If you have something to offer them that is not spammy, offer it. (I always give free advice to my new connections on their LinkedIn profiles, and many people write back either thanking me or asking me for more information about my services.) If you think it would be useful, go ahead and set up a phone or in-person meeting to get to know your new connection.

I have had success reaching out to executive coaches to let them know who I am and ask if they find it useful to have executive resume writers in their network. If they are members of the Forbes Council, I mention that in my message to them. The majority of coaches I reach out to accept my connection request, and many of them set up meetings with me. Here are some messages that have worked for me:

> Hi [first name], I see you're a member of the Forbes Coaches Council. I'm an executive resume writer and think we could be valuable connections for each other! I look forward to having you in my LinkedIn network.

Or, even simpler:

> Hi [first name], thank you for your contribution to the recent Forbes article about the future of Executive coaching. I'd love to connect!
>
> Sincerely,
> Brenda Bernstein
> Executive Resume Writer
> Author of *How to Write a KILLER LinkedIn Profile* & *How to Write a STELLAR Executive Resume*

If they accept my request, I follow up with this:

> Thanks for connecting with me, [first name]! I'm wondering, do you find connections with Executive Resume Writers to be valuable? I have some Executive coaches in my network who send clients to me, and I'd love to be a resource to you. Let's chat about how I can support your clients!
>
> Best,
> Brenda

My aim is not to be pushy but to provide value. So far it's working. A couple of the coaches I've reached out to have hired me themselves. The main lesson here is that as long as you use your networks wisely and politely, your approach can reap big rewards!

Receiving Messages

Be sure you set your email frequency under Settings & Privacy & Communications to receive individual emails for each message you get from a connection:

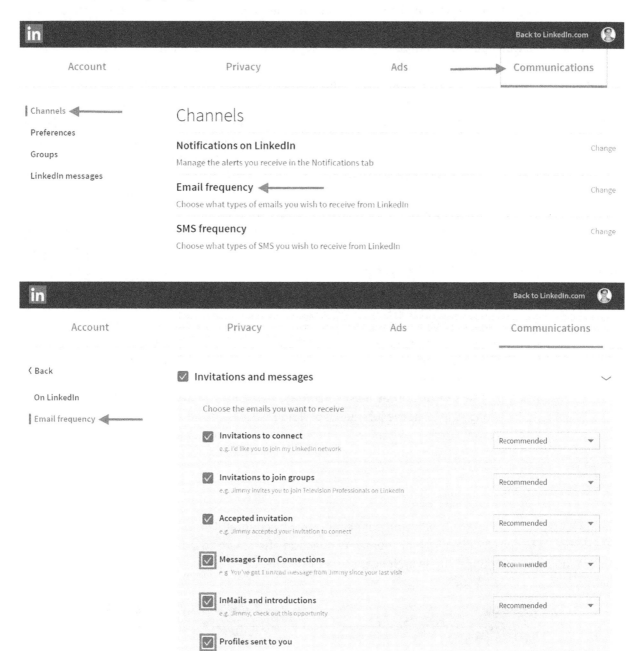

It's unclear what the "Recommended" frequency is, but you can also opt for individual (as messages arrive) and weekly.

Note that messages coming from LinkedIn might sometimes get caught by your spam filter, and if you use Gmail, messages from connections can get filtered into the "Social" category, so be sure to check these places often and don't miss that next opportunity. And sometimes, the notification system simply fails, which means you won't get notifications of your messages. So check your actual LinkedIn inbox regularly. Put it on your calendar.

What do those messages in your inbox look like? As of October 2018, LinkedIn no longer includes the full message text from connections in their email notifications for regular LinkedIn messages. The body of the email simply reads "You have 1 new message"—along with the connection's head shot and partial headline. You will need to click "View Message" to find out what your connection wants to talk about. Many people are not happy with this change, but for now it is the state of affairs.

How can you get full messages from your connections, or make sure they receive full messages from you without having to click through to LinkedIn? As much as I wish it weren't so, LinkedIn Premium is the answer. If you receive an inMail, you'll get the entire text of the message.

Similarly, if you send an inMail, your recipient will see your entire message in their inbox. Unfortunately for those who don't want to add a $59 monthly expense to their budget, LinkedIn Premium is becoming more and more necessary for a positive LinkedIn experience.

> * **Potential Issue Receiving Message Notifications:** LinkedIn Premium messages reliably generate notifications in your email inbox. With non-InMail messages, I have from time to time experienced problems with getting notified by email, even though I have my settings set to send me an email notification each time I get a message. So to be safe, **check your LinkedIn inbox on the site or app at least once/day**; and check more frequently if you're engaged in an active job search or doing business development where a quick response can make the difference between winning or losing a sale.

Let's Get Personal!

Two great ways to keep in touch with your connections are by congratulating them on their successes and wishing them a happy birthday. A simple human connection often leads to a deeper conversation. Start by checking up on what's happening in their lives using the Notifications tab:

On this page you will see the recent happy events in your connections' lives. You can customize which notifications you want to see. Just click the three dots and turn that type of notification off if you don't want it.

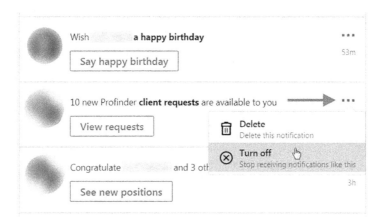

If you change your mind, turn them on again at any time by clicking "Edit" in the left sidebar.

When you see an announcement that you want to respond to, go ahead and reach out! Just click the message link to "Say happy birthday" or "Say congrats," etc.:

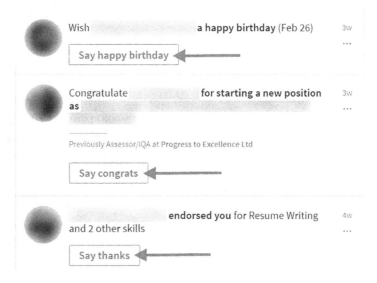

Add your customized note and send!

Other notifications you can respond to are the emails you receive letting you know your connections were mentioned in the news. What a great opportunity to congratulate them or comment on the content of the article.

Linked in™

Connections In The News

Kristy Wallace
prweb.com · 6 days ago

Freddie Mac Joins Ellevate Network

"We are very pleased to have Freddie Mac as a Corporate Partner," said Kristy Wallace, President of Ellevate Network. "Their commitment to diversity and providing professional women with the opportunities they need to succeed makes them a great fit to work with Ellevate Network. We ...

Message Kristy · Share · Wrong Person?

Laura M. Labovich
forbes.com · 1 day ago

How To Stand Out In The Job Market When You've Been In The Same Role For Years

- Laura M. Labovich, The Career Strategy Group The best way to look for a job is not to! To stand out from the crowd and create a platform where your skills and expertise will be seen. Leverage the power of social media to produce thought leadership in the form of blogs, tweets...

Message Laura M. · Share · Wrong Person?

Messaging Options

When you send a message through LinkedIn mail, you can attach files to your reply, so if you are a job seeker, you might choose to forward a copy of your resume or other marketing materials. If you are a business owner, you might attach a brochure or PowerPoint. You can also ask the person you're messaging to send something to you. I frequently request people's resumes through LinkedIn, since I offer resume writing services. Here's what the interface looks like:

Desktop View

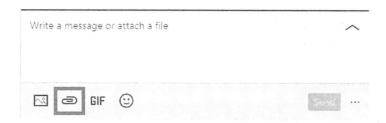

Mobile View

You can also utilize LinkedIn's new Voice Messaging feature, available in the mobile app.

In theory, this tool is a very useful way to make sure the intention of your message is understood, avoiding the potential miscommunications of written communications.

The voice messaging feature does have its downsides. One author makes a good point stating, "When someone sees a voice message, there's no way to discern the content. They have no idea what they're about to listen to . . ." Therefore, connections who don't know you might not take the time to listen to your voice message. Then again, curiosity is a strong force. It might be a good idea to preface your voice message with a written message just to be safe.

To use the voice message feature, click on the Messaging icon in the top right.

Click the plus icon to begin composing a message, then select the microphone icon at the bottom of your message window.

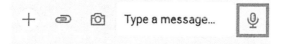

Hold down the microphone/record button while speaking. When you're finished you will have the option to send or cancel your message. Unfortunately, previewing your recording is not currently an option, so make sure you feel confident with your message before hitting send.

To learn more about voice messaging, read LinkedIn's blog article [38].

Taking it Off Line

Most important, don't be afraid to pick up the phone and talk to your new connections in real time.
     Start up a conversation and you will learn much more than you could ever gather from their profile. With LinkedIn's calendar feature, you can even suggest some available times to meet. To do so, start a new message and click the plus sign to view all of your mobile messaging features. Click on "Availability."

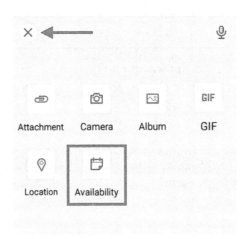

Select a few time slots from your calendar that work for you, then click the check box in the upper right:

LinkedIn will pull your information into the body of the message. Personalize and send!

You can also use the Location feature to let your connection know where you are or would like to meet in the future. Just click on the map icon, type in your desired location, and click the blue arrow icon to send a map. Note that maps are sent immediately—there's no ability to add text to your message—so be sure to precede your map with a message explaining that the meeting location is on its way.

Results to Expect

Once you start using LinkedIn messages effectively and your network starts to grow, you will see an increase in the number of conversations you're having on LinkedIn, on the phone, and over coffee. People will like you because you are treating them with respect, being curious about them, and letting them know you care about them as a person.

It goes without saying that by engaging more effectively in your LinkedIn communications, you'll also see a big increase in the results you achieve. Your calendar will be as full as you want it to be. Plus you might end up feeling good about yourself and your relationships too!

Mistake #7

Sending the Dreaded Generic LinkedIn Invitation

The Problem

LinkedIn has a generic message you can send when you request a connection. DON'T DO IT!! The generic LinkedIn invitation is a pet peeve of most LinkedIn experts and business people on LinkedIn, prompting such snarkily written articles as Why I Didn't Accept Your LinkedIn Request.[39]

Take the time to write a personal note to anyone you want to connect with. Wouldn't you appreciate the same courtesy?

This problem is especially prevalent on mobile phones, where LinkedIn has made it extremely counterintuitive to send a personalized message. But you can do it! (I'll tell you a secret: I once did this myself. That big blue Connect button is just too tempting!!)

The Tune-Up

Initiating a Connection the Right Way

On your desktop, when you click "Connect" on someone's profile or next to someone's name in a search results list, you will receive the option to send a customized invitation.

You can customize this invitation	✕
LinkedIn members are more likely to accept invitations that include a personal note.	
	Add a note Send now

I strongly urge you to choose "Add a note" (even though it's less prominent on the screen) and write something here. Clicking "Send now" without customizing sends a generic invitation containing no message at all. Here is what your contact will see:

Director, Human Resources - Corporate Services at Catholic Health
◑ 2 mutual connections

Ignore   Accept

What would someone's incentive be for accepting such a generic invitation? Instead, click "Add a note" and a popup will appear:

You cannot click "Send invitation" until you have written something personal. Make an impression!

The Mobile Challenge

To send a customized invitation, go to your contact's profile and click the "More" button (do NOT click on CONNECT!!):

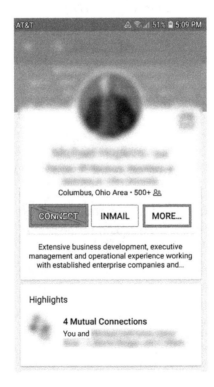

Then click "Personalize Invite":

And write your message.

Oops!!

If you accidentally connect with someone without including a message, you can always cancel the invitation or, if you miss the window for cancellation, you can send another message with a customized invitation later. Note that this second solution will only work for people who accept non-InMail messages, or if you are able to send InMail!

To rescind your invitation before it's accepted, click on the "My Network" tab:

Next, click "Manage all" in the upper right-hand corner:

On the resulting page, click on Sent and you'll get a list of pending invitations. You can click on Withdraw to cancel that message you sent accidentally.

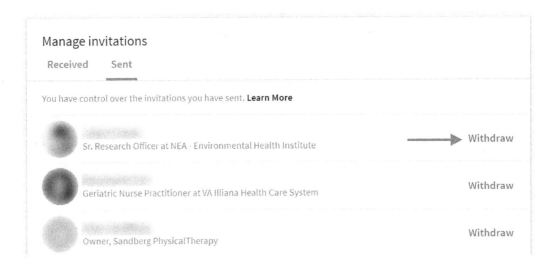

Note that you will not be able to send an invitation to that member again for up to three weeks.

Now that you know the basics about LinkedIn invitations, here's a chance to practice . . . Go to https://www.linkedin.com/in/brendabernstein to connect with me on LinkedIn!

Results to Expect

You won't get reported for spam or blocked by users, and you will have a much higher quality LinkedIn network. People will like you a **lot** more!

SECTION 2

Writing and Presentation Tips for Your KILLER LinkedIn Profile

I'm about to make suggestions that might inspire you to change some sections of your profile. If you don't want these changes announced to all your connections, go to your Settings & Privacy page, Privacy tab, and turn **"Sharing profile edits"** to **No**. While an announcement might still go out when you turn your activity updates back on, your connections will not receive notifications of every change you make while your notifications are off.

To turn off your profile change announcements, go to Settings & Privacy:

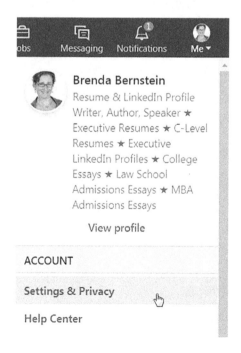

At this point you may be required to enter your password again before proceeding. You will then be taken to the Settings & Privacy page. On the Privacy tab, under "Blocking and hiding," you will see the option "Sharing profile edits":

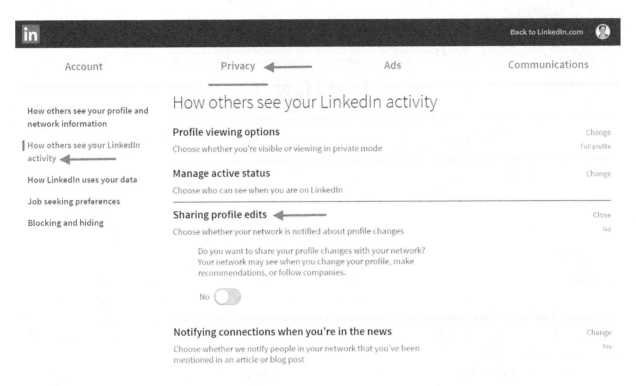

Move the switch to Yes or No depending on your preference. Then edit away!

Mistake #8

Blank or Ineffective Summary Section

The Summary section is your first opportunity to write a bio or other statement about who you are. It will get people interested in who you are and what you have to offer. The Summary is your chance to show what makes you unique and desirable. It's also your chance to give context to the rest of your profile. You have 2,000 characters to work with in this section, the first 200-230 or so of which will appear when people view your profile on desktop, and the first 100 or so of which will appear on the mobile app.

The Problem

If you don't catch your reader's attention in the first few lines of your Summary, you've lost the game. If you've done all the work to appear in a search, what's the point if you lose the attention of the people who are actually interested in reading your profile?

Leaving the Summary section blank leaves your readers with no background, and maybe no reason to read further. According to LinkedIn spokesperson May Chow, if your Summary is less than 40 words, it won't even be included in searches! Even if you use the 2,000 characters, writing long blocky paragraphs or a generally dull Summary will bore your readers at best, and turn them off at worst.

Did you copy the Summary section from your resume straight into your LinkedIn profile? When you do this, you miss out on a chance to tell your story in 2,000 characters. A copy and paste job will look exactly like a copy and paste job. I invite you to see some samples of how to do it differently on my LinkedIn Summary samples page.[40]

Another common mistake I see people make in their LinkedIn profiles is that they do not distinguish who *they* are from who their *company* is. I call this "conflating" yourself with your company.[41] It leaves your readers confused.

And then there are the drab, boring Summary statements that turn the reader off in the first sentence—the most important sentence in your entire profile!

> **Important:** If your Summary does not utilize the 2,000 characters allotted, you limit your opportunities to include keywords that can make you appear more frequently in searches. Don't let that opportunity pass you by!

The Tune-Up

To hold the attention of your readers, write not only a keyword-rich Summary, but one that makes your audience want to know more about you. It can be an engaging bio or other well-written statement about your strengths, skills and accomplishments, and what you have to contribute to your intended audience.

Make sure you are gearing this statement toward your targeted readers. If you aren't sure of your target audience, it might be because you are unclear of your direction, or because you have two very disparate audiences—in which case you might not be ready to write a Summary at all.

My only rules about the LinkedIn Summary section, if you choose to write one, are to write it with your intended audience in mind and make sure it expresses who you are and what you have to offer. Or, in the words of Catherine Byers Breet, "Who are you, and why should I care?"

Some questions you might want to answer in your LinkedIn Summary include:

- How did you get to where you are professionally?

- What are your top 3 accomplishments?

- What is the most important thing your audience should know about you and/or your company?

- What makes you different than others who do the same type of work?

- What action do you want people to take after reading your Summary?

Again, and I can't emphasize this enough: Direct your Summary to your audience! You would write something very different to target a potential employer than you would to target a potential client.

And . . . I quote Byers Breet again here:

"Dare to have a little fun! Times have changed, and people love to see a little personality and humor jump off their screens when they are learning about you. Keep it light, clean and professional . . . but dare to let a little of yourself shine through."

Following are some issues that might come up as you are writing your LinkedIn Summary, and some ideas of how to address them.

1st or 3rd Person?

Most LinkedIn summaries are written in the first person ("I"), which makes them more personal and conversational. Some higher-level executives prefer to write in the 3rd person ("He" or "She"). In the end, this is your decision. Look at some profiles similar to yours and see what you like best!

Regardless of whether you write in first or third person, your Summary must express who you are as a *person*. Your company website, your LinkedIn Company page and even the LinkedIn Experience section are available for reporting information about your company. Your Summary is there for LinkedIn members to learn more about *you*!

How to Start?

With the new interface that LinkedIn rolled out in early 2017, only the first 200-230 characters (including spaces) are visible when you initially view someone's profile. This means that whatever you consider the most important information for viewers needs to be in your first few sentences.

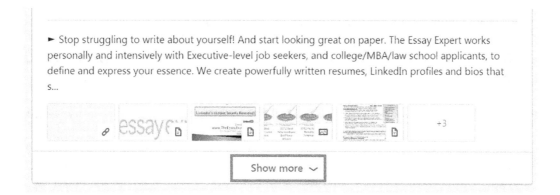

> ► Stop struggling to write about yourself! And start looking great on paper. The Essay Expert works personally and intensively with Executive-level job seekers, and college/MBA/law school applicants, to define and express your essence. We create powerfully written resumes, LinkedIn profiles and bios that s...

It also means that contrary to older-style LinkedIn summaries, you don't want to start with a line across the page. " ——————— ." Graphics here will just take up valuable realestate.

If you attract enough interest in your opening lines, people will click on "See more" to read the rest of your summary.

I often choose to start the Summary section with a sub-headline. Even though you have a headline for your profile, attention spans are short so it can't hurt to remind people of who you are. Don't use the exact wording from your headline; instead create something new that includes keywords and a tagline. While this is not a rule, it's a trick to put in your toolbox.

If you're up against writer's block, try looking at other profiles of people in your industry. You might get inspired! Don't copy their profiles word for word of course—that would be plagiarism—but you can use them as jumping off points.

Example #1: IT Professional

Headline:
Senior Software Architect | Systems Automation | Cloud Solutions | Systems Management / Integration | Data Management

Summary Intro:
SENIOR SYSTEMS ANALYST AND PROGRAMMER WITH LINUX AND CLOUD SOLUTIONS EXPERTISE

Example #2: Compliance Executive

Headline:
INTERNATIONAL COMPLIANCE EXECUTIVE | Risk Management | Investigation Leadership | Compliance Strategies | Loss Control

Summary Intro:
11 YEARS OF OPERATIONAL TURNAROUNDS, REVENUE GROWTH, FRAUD/WASTE CONTROL AND COST-CUTTING | EMEA, NORTH AMERICA, AND LATIN AMERICA.

Following your headline, you have many choices.
You might choose to list some of your competencies. For example:

GLOBAL FINANCE EXECUTIVE AND ENTREPRENEUR with 20 years' success in opening new markets, creating new services, and building new companies.

Product Development | Key Decision Maker Relationships | Market and Regulatory Trends | Emerging Markets | Process Development | Strategies

Or you might choose to dive right into your history:

I am a Ph.D. candidate in Computer Engineering with 12+ years of systems architecture design, software development, and process enhancement experience in the US and abroad. A strategic and informed risk taker, I am an effective project manager and the "go-to" choice to analyze complex problems and identify actionable processes.

OR, if using 3rd person:

SENIOR-LEVEL MANAGER & CAPACITY BUILDER • SITE REPLICATION EXPERT • PROVEN LEADER OF PEOPLE & PROJECTS

Michelle Henry has almost 20 years of progressive experience in business, community, and program development and cultivates prosperous organizations. She recently served as Senior Vice President at a large, national non-profit and has held positions with United Way of NYC and the Center for Alternative Sentencing & Employment Services.

I have seen effective profiles that begin with a quotation. For instance, this one from Eric Schmidt, VP of Business Technology at Spacesaver Corporation:

"You need to be constantly reinventing. You need to challenge things. You need to try different ideas, different technologies, different creative approaches. Because the world is changing." Miles Nadal. That quote is very representative of my career . . .

There is no hard and fast rule about how to start your profile. Choose a strategy and style that works for you!

Run-On Sentences

Run-on sentences can leave us both out of breath and confused. It's worth taking some time to write a Summary that comes across clearly and concisely. Use powerful language and correct grammar. It makes a difference.

You vs. Your Company

One of the biggest mistakes I see in LinkedIn summaries is the tendency for business owners to mix up who they are and who their company is. They might, for instance, write one sentence about the company followed by a sentence about themselves. The reader is left confused.

Here's an example from Michael Phelps (no, not the swimmer), who does a great job of distinguishing himself from his company, and who succeeds in selling both:

> I am a research professional and LinkedIn trainer with more than eight years of combined market intelligence, competitive intelligence and Internet recruiting experience. My focus has been on deep web sourcing, executive interviews and online networking through social media. I've spoken at more than 60 events to hundreds of business professionals about the power of LinkedIn!

See how this entire paragraph is about the *person* himself? It works! We're right there with him! His second section reads as follows:

> Current Phelps Research Services Initiatives:
>
> * Selling and conducting targeted business research to help Wisconsin-based sales teams utilize market, competitive and prospect information to customize approaches to their clients.
>
> * Selling and conducting customized LinkedIn training to sales, marketing, legal, HR, public relations, consulting, research and training teams.

Phelps clearly makes a switch from talking about himself to talking about his company. We understand, since his last name is Phelps, that he is the principal in the company and that he is behind these initiatives. We stay engaged and want to read more.

Here's another example of a business owner who writes about himself while still making it clear what his company offers:

> LEADERSHIP DEVELOPMENT • BUSINESS STRATEGY • MANAGEMENT CONSULTING •
> Is your business poised to blast above your current expectations? Are you ready to take action to heighten your leadership performance?
>
> For more than two decades, I have helped executives improve success ratios, productivity, ROI and ROE. My clients include Fortune 500 companies such as Crown Holdings, IBM, and Time Warner, as well as many smaller business entities.
>
> When problems and obstacles go unsolved, they prevent optimal operations and results. Asking and answering precisely the right questions is sometimes all it takes to develop a leader's ability to identify and resolve a business dilemma.
>
> That's where I step in. In addition to consulting and mentoring executives and entrepreneurs, I have served as CEO of four companies, where I have improved leadership

practices, implemented significant efficiencies, increased lines of credit, and preserved relationships through pragmatic and compassionate management.

My unique and confidential approach of guided dialogue and best practices teaches leaders to lead themselves so they get their careers back on track. Work with me to work smarter. Reduce stress by conquering challenges such as . . .

- Distractions
- Low Productivity
- Employee Retention
- Overdue Work
- Out-of-control Budgets
- Mismanaged Projects

Leaders who manage these issues in turn drive their company to solve problems and create higher levels of individual and organizational productivity. Most important, they become free to enjoy business again.

For more information about my company [Company Name], please visit [Web address] or read my book, Stop Telling . . . Start Leading! The Art of Managing People by Asking Questions.

When you are ready to take action to improve your leadership performance, call 555.555.1234 for a conversation about your requirements.

Confidential Job Search?

If you are engaged in a confidential job search, it is essential that your LinkedIn Summary does not make you look like a job seeker. I am unable to share specific examples of profiles for confidential job seekers, for obvious reasons. However, here are some things to keep in mind and some guidelines to follow:

1. Remember, recruiters love passive job seekers! If you write a profile that sells your current company well, makes it clear you are happy and thriving in your current position, and includes effective keywords, guess what? You WILL be contacted by recruiters (assuming you follow most of the other advice in this book). And you could make your current employer happy as well—maybe even attract new clients and alliances.

2. Turn off your activity broadcasts before making any changes. Please see **Mistake #18** for instructions on how to change your privacy settings so that you do not announce to the whole world that you have changed your profile. Many employers see changes in your profile as a sign that you might be looking; so if this is not cool with your current employer, turn off your notifications!

3. You might want to stick with talking about what you do for your current company. The more emphasis you put on what you're currently doing, the more you will benefit your current employer.

4. You can also go with a general bio format. Just talk about where you've come from and how you got to where you are now.

5. Limit the number of "accomplishment" bullets in your Summary. Bullets of accomplishments scream out "resume" and might raise suspicion.

Be cautious about using LinkedIn's Open Candidates. All recruiters will be able to see that you are open for opportunities, so word could potentially make it back to your current employer. See **Mistake #16** for more details about this LinkedIn Jobs feature.

Let's Get Personal

Some of the best profile summaries highlight the personalities of the people writing them. Following are some samples that stood out to me for their creative approach.

Example #1: Anna Wang, Diabetes Sales Specialist (check out her last line!)

Quota-Beating, Award Winning Sales Rep |

I am an extremely effective communicator, and an incredibly fast learner. I enjoy rising to new challenges, and I thrive under pressure.

I close deals.

I have an innate ability to read between the lines and identify the needs of my customers, allowing me to consistently exceed quotas with my high close ratio and high rate of account retention.

When training reps in the field, I can quickly spot their weaknesses, and devise an immediately actionable plan to increase their close ratio.

As an ADM, selling four days a week, I broke $300K in revenue in 2013 to rank #10 out of 250 nationwide.

When I'm not bludgeoning quotas with a baseball bat, I can be found rocking out with my band, or parked at a poker table.

Example #2: Jess Hornyak, Marketing Director

When I was little, I wanted to drive a garbage truck. Then, I moved to Wisconsin and declared I would be the next Green Bay Packers QB once Brett Favre retired.

No one ever told me "No" (or that girls don't play in the NFL), but soon after I found art and writing, and hopes of being the next big name in football were passed along to Aaron Rodgers.

Ever since I've been immersed in the arts: from Saturday morning watercolor lessons and hand-made art projects for my friends' birthday gifts, to falling in love with writing and producing a novel for an 8th grade project and a minor in creative writing from a Big Ten school.

I've filled just as many notebooks with poems and imaginative free writing exercises as I have canvases with brush strokes.

I'm also practical. I make lists. I played three sports since I was three, and learned from a young age how to manage my time. I hated losing, and still do. Saying I'm competitive is an understatement. I want to give my best all the time, in hopes of inspiring others to be better too. And, not only am I a team player as a result, but I've come to believe that being a team player is at the center of any type of success. Because it's true when they say that two minds are better than one.

Therefore, it's safe to say I don't fit into a traditional bubble. I'm an art director, but I'm really so much more. I'm a strategist. A writer. An artist. A competitor. It's why I'm looking for people who could use a little more non-traditional in their everyday lives.

Plus, it means I'm never bored. And definitely not boring.

I moved to Austin, Texas to get a Masters degree and complete the prestigious Texas Creative sequence. I have two degrees and ample real-world experience. Now, I just need a place to use it.

Specialties: Advertising, brand management, brochure design, website production, budgeting, closing, coaching, concept development, customer service, development, Adobe Photoshop, Dreamweaver, Illustrator, InDesign, Microsoft Excel, Microsoft PowerPoint, Microsoft Word

How would you express your true self in your LinkedIn Summary? It might not look like either of the above examples, and, in fact, it shouldn't! If you're inspired to get creative, find your own expression and go for it! Remember to include as many keywords as you can in the process.

What Makes a Good Call to Action? And Should I Include Contact Info?

If you want readers of your profile to take action, then tell them so! Ask them to contact you if you want to enter into conversations about a particular topic. Tell them that you can create results like the ones reported in your profile for their company.

If you are in a confidential job search, your best call to action would be something relating to your current company—perhaps an action for a potential client to take.

Example #1:

If you would like to connect with a top-level cross-functional leader on the forefront of global business technology, particularly the industry shift to Cloud Services and Channel Incentives models, send me an invite!

Example #2:

I am available for a leadership role where I can leverage my expertise to build new brands and transform businesses for rapid growth.

SET UP A FREE CONSULTATION TODAY!

Should you include contact information in your Summary?

If you are a job seeker wanting recruiters to access your contact information readily, or if you want people in general to be able to contact you easily, then you might want to include your contact information in the first 50 words of your Summary. Why? Because the list view generated by LinkedIn® Recruiter displays the beginning of your Summary section. If your contact information shows up in the list view, recruiters won't have to work hard to reach you.

You can also put your contact information at the conclusion of your Summary, which is where people will look if their interest was sparked enough to read through to the end.

You can use cute Unicode symbols before your email address and phone number, like this:

Contact me: ☏ 123-456-7890 or ✉ my.email.address [at] gmail.com.

If you do include your email address, consider writing [at] instead of @ so that spambots won't be able to find your address easily.

Remember, you also have the option to include your contact details in the Contact Information section. See **Mistake #3** for more on how to do that.

Name with Common Misspellings?

If you have a commonly misspelled name, include common misspellings in your Summary. So if your name is Izabela Tomkins, include in your summary a line that says "Izabela Tomkins, AKA Isabella Thompkins." That way you will appear in searches for common misspellings of your name!

Other Special Issues?

For samples from the LinkedIn® Official Blog of possible ways to approach career changes and other gaps on your LinkedIn profile, see their presentation on SlideShare, Representing your unique career path on your LinkedIn profile:[42]

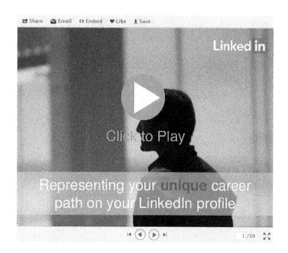

Even with all these topics and suggestions addressed, you may have a career history that requires individual attention. Don't be afraid to ask friends, colleagues or other professionals for assistance and feedback.

Results to Expect

A well-written or even creatively written Summary tells the world that you are taking control over your personal brand. By powerfully stating who you are and what you have to offer up front, you will encourage more people to read your full profile. Add to that a solid showing of keywords and a robust network, and more people will not just find you but also read your profile. A well-directed and well-placed call to action is the final ingredient and is likely to inspire more people to pick up the phone or send you an email.

According to Link Humans, "a summary of 40 words or more makes you more likely to turn up in a future employer's search." And LinkedIn® Small Business states that profiles with summaries get 10 times more views. Your Summary CAN be the section that gets you a job or a new customer! It is not a section to be ignored.

SAMPLES

For samples of LinkedIn Summary sections from one of The Essay Expert's clients, see my LinkedIn Summary samples page.[43] You might also like my blog article, 3 Reasons NOT to Copy Your Resume into Your LinkedIn Summary Section.[44]

Following are some additional LinkedIn Profile Summaries by The Essay Expert. These samples are geared toward the U.S. job market where a strong sell is appropriate; adjust accordingly based on your target country.

Example #1

Ross Dabrow

VP / Director of Sales | Startup, Turnaround & Growth Expert |
High-Tech Sales & Digital Content Licensing

LAUNCHING / TRANSFORMING BUSINESSES DOMESTICALLY AND INTERNATIONALLY

✓ **Building #1 sales organizations.**

With a servant leadership philosophy, I have repeatedly proven that when sales executives invest in assembling and training teams of emotionally intelligent strategic thinkers aligned with the company vision, revenue & sales performance follow.

After 13 years of driving explosive growth in digital / online media—most recently as VP of Sales at T3Media (formerly Thought Equity Motion), a global video management / content licensing leader—I know what it takes to rescue failing businesses, achieve 180-degree turnarounds and guide startups to market dominance in E-Commerce & B2B environments.

✓ **Applying high-velocity, decisive business leadership when organizations need to power launches or overcome a crisis.**

After delivering historic-level sales at Getty Images, I was recruited by Thought Equity Motion and positioned this no-name startup to ▶ overpower the top 2 industry players and ascend to market leadership in our initial 24 months sales-startup. After 5 years at other firms, I was re-recruited and ▶ transformed their troubled Eastern sales operation into the highest-performing region in 1 year.

✓ **Channeling forward-thinking creativity into YoY revenue growth.**

At Framepool, a German media rights company with no U.S. brand awareness, I optimized tight resources to pioneer a product that offset flatlining sales and attracted formerly elusive ad agency business. We converted every single customer-facing meeting into sales, ▶ outdistanced 4 formidable competitors to earn "preferred vendor" status and ▶ realized triple-digit growth in 3 years.

Reach out if you are looking to connect with a SENIOR SALES EXECUTIVE who delivers game-changing impact on sales organizations and the top line.

Example #2

Jim Masloski

Customs Brokerage Leader | Director-Client Technology | Import/Export |
Process Improvement | Customer Service

TENACIOUS, PERFORMANCE-DRIVEN CUSTOMS BROKERAGE LEADER -
Streamlining processes and providing the highest level of service to customers.

Since 1996 I have been with Norman G. Jensen, Inc. (NGJ), a major provider of U.S. and Canadian customs brokerage, freight forwarding, warehousing, distribution, and consulting services to thousands of North American importers and exporters. During this time I have built a well-rounded background that touches all facets of the business in an Automated Commercial Environment.

EXCELLENCE AT NGJ

▶ At NGJ, we take great pride in adding value to our customers' cross-border trade by ensuring that their products are smoothly and expeditiously moved across the borders of North America.

▶ We provide the most complete U.S./Canadian border coverage in the industry, as well as an impressive array of software solutions for small, medium, and large importers and exporters.

Currently I am the Southern Border Regional Manager and Automation & Centralization Director of our processing center in Sioux Falls, SD, where I manage all electronic customer communications and play a key role in directing operations, production, customer service, and new business development. I am able to talk to a farmer in the field about the most efficient way to get his product across the border and am equally comfortable making a presentation on process improvements to Senior Executives.

INNOVATION AND EFFICIENCY CONTRIBUTIONS:

▶ Initiated, presented, and directed the implementation of process improvements from cradle to grave, including the development of software to improve processes for cross-border trade.

▶ Using my unique ability to work the simplest task through to the end product, whether it is a project or procedures, I am skilled at developing software and procedures that save time and reduce costs in international trade. When you need an expert in the customer brokerage industry, contact me at [phone] or [email].

Example #3

Karen Rogers

Executive well-versed in Strategic Planning, Capacity Building, Program Implementation & Partnership Development

SENIOR-LEVEL MANAGER & CAPACITY BUILDER ◆ SITE REPLICATION EXPERT ◆ PROVEN LEADER OF PEOPLE & PROJECTS

Karen Rogers has almost 20 years of progressive experience in business, community, and program development and cultivates prosperous organizations. She recently served as Senior Vice President at a large, national non-profit and has held positions with United Way of NYC and the Center for Alternative Sentencing & Employment Services.

Karen's success is derived from her abilities to leverage stakeholder relationships; manage multi-city initiatives; develop partnerships; and achieve results through innovation. She takes a project from zero to full speed ahead, fostering high-performing teams and uniting senior management. Her unique ability to build capacities of scale ensures fiscal responsibility and business growth.

Demonstrating leadership in community service is also a priority for Karen. She served as Chair of the Board at the Center for Community Alternatives and currently contributes as a Board Member on CCA's audit committee. Further, she has presented on benefits access at national conferences.

CAREER HIGHLIGHTS:

» **PROGRAM GROWTH**—Replicated proven benefits access model that originated in New York and expanded it across 8 states.

» **FISCAL MANAGEMENT**—Oversaw $14 million government- and private-sector-funded portfolio of work support programs, including public and private benefits, housing and foreclosure mitigation, and conditional cash transfers.

» **PERFORMANCE MANAGEMENT**—Managed more than 40 employees, volunteers and consultants to collectively deliver vital services to low income workers and their families.

» **CAPACITY BUILDING**—Increased capacity of nonprofits nationally to integrate benefits access services into their program designs. Organizations searching for a transformative leader will find their ideal candidate in Karen Rogers.

Example #4:

Paul F Hatch

Engineering Project Manager • Power Generation/Distribution • Marine Propulsion • Commercial Facility Management • CPE

Commissioning Startup Engineer | Full Cycle Project Management | Hands-on Technical Expertise | Matrix Team Leadership | RFP Response | Troubleshooting | Dispute Resolution | Customer Satisfaction | Cost & Revenue Optimization | Budget & Resource Management | HVAC | Boilers | Marine Diesel| Electrical Systems | Automation

LARGE POWER PROJECT COMMISSIONING/STARTUP
√ Georgia Pacific Port Hudson: 1.2M lbs/hr (Process)
√ Roquette America: 630,000M lbs/hr (Process)
√ Howe Sound Pulp and Paper: 280,000M lbs/hr (Process)
√ Gainesville Renewable Energy Center: 100 MWE

FULL-CYCLE PROJECT MANAGEMENT: RFP, NEGOTIATIONS, DELIVERY
√ $100K building automation system digital controller design/upgrade for lower utility costs.
√ Solid chemical Nalco 3D Tracer system installation with 18-month payback.

TROUBLESHOOTING & REPAIRS
√ Design/installation of high temperature knife gate valves for bed ash drain to replace ball valves, saving $30K in annual repairs.
√ Analysis of high temperature vessel head cracking problem, location of design flaw, and implementation of design changes to save $15K in annual welding costs.

REVENUE GENERATION
√ Over $900K revenue for service and parts in 6 years.

TRAINING
√ 95% training success rate for both new and existing staff.

EDUCATION:
• BSET, Calhoon MEBA Engineering School
• Graduate Certificate, HVAC, Systems Design and Building Controls, Northeastern University

CERTIFICATIONS DOE
• Pump Specialist (PSAT)
• Steam System Specialist
• Demand Side Management Specialist

ASSOCIATION OF FACILITIES ENGINEERING (AFE)
• Certified Plant Engineer (CPE) OSHA
• 10 Hour Certification

LICENSING
• US Coast Guard license, Motor and Steam Vessels, Unlimited Horsepower, all endorsements including VSO, STCW,TWIC and Gas Turbines
• Commonwealth of Massachusetts certification, First Class Steam Engineer (Unlimited Horsepower)

I am eager to hear about opportunities for leading large field or marine engineering projects. Please feel free to contact me.

Example #5:

Albert R. Crimaldi, MBA

Hospitality | Hotel & Resort Management | Sales | Reservations | Marketing | Events | Manager | Operations | Accounting

◆ PASSION FOR HOTEL INDUSTRY | TOP-NOTCH HOSPITALITY EXPERIENCE ◆

Since the start of my career in hospitality as a guest service agent, I have worked in every aspect of the industry–from catering & event management to sales, marketing, revenue, accounting & operations.
I'm known as a high-energy, decisive problem-solver with a zeal for creating well-considered, efficient operations. What makes me excel in my field:

HIGHLY ANALYTICAL, PENSIVE & DECISIVE MIND

◆ Conducted full-spectrum industry/financial analyses of businesses.

◆ Devised/implemented grand opening operations for 65,000 sq. ft. entertainment venue; created employee handbook, surveyed post-launch procedures, established sustainable business solutions.

◆ Spearheaded innovative marketing strategies to bolster sales for multi-property management firm.

◆ Adept at improving guest satisfaction and employee satisfaction scores.

WELL-ROUNDED BACKGROUND: PROFESSIONAL, ACADEMIC, TECHNICAL

◆ Professional experience in hotel, resort, and rental management. Consistently among the Top regional sellers for rental management firm.

◆ Graduate studies in economics, accounting, marketing research, quantitative analysis, business and finance. Ongoing professional development.

◆ Proficient in MS Office applications; experience with Delphi, Opera, Synxis, Easy RMS, Smith Travel Research, Epitome, Micros, and Fidelio.

SUPERIOR TIME MANAGEMENT

◆ Worked full-time while completing top-ranked MBA program for Hospitality in the U.S.

◆ Managed 100-person staff and planned dozens of weekly events while supervising all retail operations at busy entertainment complex.

◆ Handled reservations, supervised personnel, monitored customer service, and fielded inquiries for 2 high-traffic luxury hotel properties simultaneously.

Specialties:

◆ Hospitality | Hotels | Resorts | Tourism | Sales | Marketing Strategy | Events

◆ Business Analysis & Development | Relationship Management | Accounting | Finance |Revenue Analysis & Management | Operations | Operational Forecasting

◆ Employee Training | Policies & Procedures | Efficiency | Team Building

◆ World Travel - I have visited: Dublin, Ireland | London, England | Florence, Rome & Naples, Italy | Paris & Aix en Provence, France | Montreal, Quebec City, Toronto, Canada

---

You might still want assistance writing your LinkedIn Summary. After all, writing about yourself is one of the hardest things you will ever have to do! The Essay Expert offers professional services to create a Summary that is uniquely about you. We ask you questions, interview you, and write the Summary for you, complete with graphics that you can cut and paste into your profile.

See **Appendix K** for coupon codes and to read what clients are saying about our LinkedIn Profile Services.

You are now halfway through your 18 steps to a KILLER LinkedIn profile! Like us on Facebook for more suggestions and to join a community of like-minded readers. Please share your comments . . . online!

Mistake #9

No Descriptions or Weak Descriptions of Job Duties and Accomplishments

The Problem

People are looking at your LinkedIn profile to find out what you've done professionally. If you don't tell them, they might be left wondering what you are hiding, or whether you're just too lazy to write something. You are also losing out on opportunities to insert keywords into your profile.

The Tune-Up

For an effective Experience section, provide robust descriptions for your most recent and relevant jobs. Note: You are not required to match your resume exactly to your LinkedIn profile. Since you have the option of *attaching* your resume to your profile (see **Mistake #15**), you can use the Experience section on LinkedIn to complement rather than duplicate what's on the resume.

To add a position to your Experience section, go to your profile page, scroll down to find your Experience section, and then click the plus icon:

Note that when adding a new position, you can choose whether or not to notify your network:

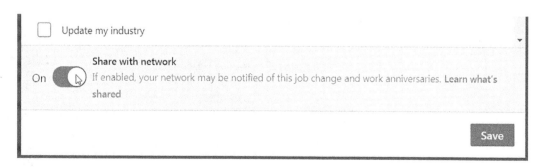

When you fill in your company, if the entity has a LinkedIn Company Page, that listing should appear as you begin typing the name.

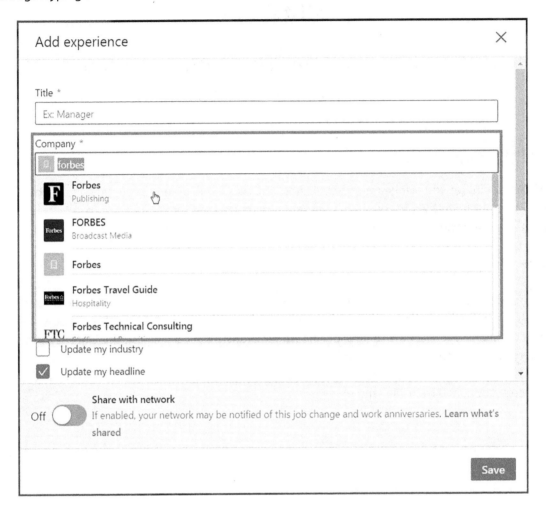

Once you have saved your entry, the company's logo will also appear on your profile beside the name. Companies that are established on LinkedIn add credibility to your work history.

A recent LinkedIn study[45] found that members with current positions get up to 5 times more connection requests. So be sure to complete a current position.

You can rearrange the entries within your Experience section by dragging and dropping the four black bars to the right of the entry. These bars will appear when you hover over the position. Note, however, that not all entries can be reordered. For instance, if you have 2 positions that are [date] to Present, you can rearrange them. If there are no black bars, the item cannot be moved.

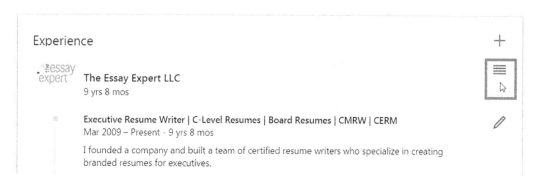

How should I show multiple roles at the same company?

There are two ways to list your promotion in your Experience section:

1. Create a new entry for each role you've held at a single company, listing them as separate positions. Remember to include keywords in your job titles!

2. Use method one, plus add another entry. In the second entry, list the full date range of your employment at the company and include as many of your positions as fit in the job title field, plus the phrase "and other positions"—for example, "Senior Product Manager, Product Manager, and other positions"; then list all your job titles in the description if they did not fit in the job title field. Your positions will technically be represented twice; however, readers will also get a sense of your full time at the company. Option #2 also gives you an opportunity to maximize the keywords in your job titles and descriptions.

3. When adding consecutive positions at the same company, LinkedIn groups them into a single section to show your progression. In other words, instead of showing as several different entries for the same company, the company will only be listed once, and your subsequent positions will appear in that section. Here's an example:

BUMBLE BEE **Bumble Bee Foods, Inc.**
3 yrs 4 mos

Vice President | Supply Chain | Integration Development
Oct 2005 – Jan 2009 · 3 yrs 4 mos
Greater San Diego Area

Vice President, Supply Chain, Operations – Integration and Development (2007-2009)
• Successfully and Under Budget, led the enterprise wide of the SAP Manufacturing Modules of PTS, WMS & QM for all of the company's main live manufacturing sites (Los Angeles, New Jersey, Maine and Puerto Rico).... See more

Vice President | Supply Chain Distribution
Oct 2005 – Aug 2006 · 11 mos

• Restructured and rejuvenated successfully, a completely dysfunctional and poorly managed distribution Segment of an accusation. reorganized large transportation segments which resulted in substantial service improvements and cost reductions.
o Reduced operating cost by more $1.2 Million, in one year.... See more

Should my Experience sections be copied from my resume?

I like to say that your LinkedIn Experience section should be completed as if you were talking to someone at a networking event. After all, LinkedIn is one big networking event! I generally prefer these sections to be written in the 1st person ("I") and to be fairly conversational, with some bullets of your accomplishments to make it clear what you're capable of achieving.

Don't forget that every section of LinkedIn is a repository for keywords! You can even put a Skills list in each of your Experience sections to beef up your search results. Sometimes, including a description of each company is an easy way to include keywords.

If you happen to be applying for a job using your LinkedIn profile, usually there is an option to attach a resume. If there is no such option, then it will be necessary for you to include all your resume bullets in your LinkedIn Experience.

For any resume-like bullets, start your phrases with verbs whenever possible (past tense verbs for past positions, present tense verbs for present positions). Rather than state your job duties, state what you accomplished or how you helped the organization you work(ed) for. The more concrete and quantifiable you are, the better (include keywords!). If you are struggling with how to write effective resume bullets, you might like my e-books, *How to Write a WINNING Resume* and *How to Write a STELLAR Executive Resume*.

Some examples of great bullets are as follows:

- Secured record $5 million order from Varian Medical that was the largest single order taken in North America. Obtained trust of Management Team to implement key strategies for success.

- Improved team effectiveness by 25% in six months by redefining sales strategy and message, developing and documenting a formal sales process, and training the group in sales skills and use of new strategy.

- Teach 4 separate LinkedIn training courses.
  - LinkedIn 101: Learning the Basics of LinkedIn
  - The Top Ten LinkedIn Business Development Strategies
  - Sourcing and Recruiting Top Talent Using LinkedIn
  - Tactical Research and Intelligence Gathering on LinkedIn

Note how these bullets leave you thinking, "It sounds like this person might be able to accomplish something for me."

Here's an example of a well-crafted LinkedIn Experience section, from The Essay Expert's client Ross Dabrow. Note that here, I break my own rule of using "I"; I break my own rules a lot!

Vice President Sales | Startup & Turnaround Leadership | Strategy Development | Change Management

T3Media (formerly Thought Equity Motion) March 2013–Present (1 year 1 month)

Dates: 2013 to Present; and 2006 to 2008 (3 Years)

▶ T3Media is an industry leader in digital content licensing and asset management.

Originally recruited in '06 by this industry startup to launch sales operations across 3 major U.S. media markets. Exerted strategic authority as VP of Sales, North America to achieve 112%+ YoY revenue growth and overtake top global market leaders in less than 2 years.

After expanding international business expertise for 5 years with other companies, received an exclusive invitation from T3Media's CEO and Head of Global Sales to return to the company, revive challenged Eastern sales division (Eastern U.S. and Canada) and restore market credibility.

▶ **SUCCESS HIGHLIGHTS** ◀

✓ Turned lowest-ranking region to highest company-wide performer within 1 year of turnaround by restructuring and leading sales organization to deliver 31% global licensing revenue.

✓ Improved monthly sales pipeline 27% via lead generation strategy.

✓ Slashed operating expenses 16% YoY by introducing efficiency controls across the region.

Sometimes lackluster bullets or descriptions in your LinkedIn profile are an indication that your resume needs an overhaul as well. If you are a job seeker, consider hiring a professional resume writer to make sure that your entire presentation—resume and LinkedIn profile—are optimized to get you interviews! The Essay Expert offers resume writing services[46] for people at all stages of their careers and we would be happy to work with you.

Again, note that while you want your resume and LinkedIn profile to be consistent with each other, you do not want your LinkedIn profile to look *exactly* like your resume. To engage the reader in a more creative way, consider writing an engaging paragraph followed by some select bullets on LinkedIn. If you are a job seeker, remember that many of the people reading your LinkedIn profile will have already seen your resume; so give your viewers something a little different to read! Also, there might be items on your resume that are too confidential to share in the public space of LinkedIn. Rather than automatically copying your resume bullets into your LinkedIn profile, consider how you want to craft each section for your audience.

Results to Expect

Your readers will be able to understand something about your experience that they would not know from reading your resume. They will feel more of a human connection with you. And they will be impressed by your accomplishments, which are an indication of what you could offer them. By learning more about you, employers or potential customers can determine whether you're someone they want to contact for further discussion.

Mistake #10

Lack of Consistency/Discrepancies in Format and Structure—and Spelling, Grammar and Punctuation Errors

The Problem

Lack of consistency makes information harder to absorb because the reader starts to expect a particular format or grammatical construction—and instead gets something else. A mixed up format also appears unprofessional; people might think you did not take the time or know enough to put care into the details. Spelling and grammatical errors will turn many of your readers off and absolutely do not project the professional image you want on LinkedIn. You can send away employers, customers and clients with a single—and **avoidable**—error. Don't let this happen to you!

The Tune-Up

Be consistent. If you have a list of items that start with verbs, make them ALL start with verbs. If you are writing in the third person (e.g., *Ms. Bernstein* is an expert writer. She holds an English degree from Yale University . . .), write everything in the third person; if you're writing in the first person (e.g., I *teach* people how to use LinkedIn effectively; I *work* with job seekers and business owners), stick to the first person. If you use periods at the end of your bullets, do it everywhere. If you have a heading under one job description that says "Major Accomplishments," use the heading in all positions where you had major accomplishments.

Whenever you add a new position to your profile, make sure you use the same structure and format as you used for past positions. If it's a new position, people will understand if it's a little shorter than positions you've held for years; but then remember to update it! Once you've been in a position for 2-3 years, you need to add accomplishments so it doesn't look like all your great achievements happened in past jobs. Staying current with your accomplishments is key.

To make sure you are staying consistent, find a good editor to review your profile! Use your friends and family if they have skills in this area.

Another effective tool is Grammarly's extension for Chrome. Grammarly will tell you the number of "errors" it finds in your writing. This number will be in a red circle in the bottom right of the box you are working in.

Grammarly is currently available for Firefox, Safari and Chrome. To learn more about Grammarly's browser extension and to install it, visit their support page[47] and search for your browser + "extension."

Be careful! Grammarly often identifies as "errors" some things that constitute perfectly good English. The program is not a substitute for your own (or an editor's) discernment.

Results to Expect

Your consistency will demonstrate that you are organized, detail-oriented, and capable of clear communication. And your viewers will easily read your entire profile. An error-free profile will have people saying, "Wow what a great profile! It's so well put together! This person presents himself/herself really well. I'm ready to take action."

Mistake #11

Unattractive Formatting

The Problem

Unattractive formatting looks unprofessional and it can make your profile hard to read. The most common formatting issue is with bullets. Does the following look attractive to you?

> • Directed $3 million dollar product division which developed solutions for FTSE 100 companies and others.
> • Successfully managed OEM technology relationships with HP, Lennox, Kyocera, Citizens and Brother.
> • Brought in new products and evaluated software development needs to maintain company's leading position in the technical world.

Even if your eyes don't hurt reading these bullets (mine do), you will probably notice that these tiny dots do not draw your attention to each statement. They are a weak formatting choice.

The Tune-Up

One of my favorite bullet formats to use on LinkedIn is the arrow: ▶
  Look at the difference:

> ▶ Directed $3 million dollar product division which developed solutions for FTSE 100 companies and others.
> ▶ Successfully managed OEM technology relationships with HP, Lennox, Kyocera, Citizens and Brother.
> ▶ Brought in new products and evaluated software development needs to maintain company's leading position in the technical world.

Now my eyes are easily drawn to each of these notable achievements rather than straining to read them. (Unfortunately, hanging indents are still not an option on LinkedIn.)
  Where can you find these symbols to insert into your profile? They do not always translate correctly from word processing programs, so feel free to copy and paste from my profile.[48] You will also find lines and other symbols you might like. "Steal" away!

You might also like these bullets:

Symbol	Unicode (Arial Unicode MS)
▣	25A3
■	25A0
◈	25C8
✦	2726
▶	25B8

To use these bullets in your LinkedIn profile, one option is to insert a symbol into a Word document and copy and paste it into your LinkedIn profile. I've found that if you use Arial Unicode MS or Lucida Sans Unicode font, the symbols usually copy correctly.

If you want to experiment with different geometric shapes, or even letters in different languages, try copying and pasting your favorites from Wikipedia's List of Unicode Characters[49] or (for foreign languages) use Google Translate.[50] Or, I recently found CopyPasteCharacter.com, where you can easily find, click and paste characters into your profile.

You can also go to your character map. If you need to know how to access your character map, Google "character map for Mac" or "character map Windows 7" (or Vista etc.). There are many sources that will help you find it. On a PC, type "character" in the windows search bar and the character map will come up. Here's what it looks like:

Next, choose the symbol you want to insert into your profile and double click on it. The symbol will appear in the "Characters to copy" box. You can double click on another character, and another, as many times as you want until you have the string of characters you want to insert:

Hit "Copy" (on the lower right) and then paste the characters into your profile.

If you are using a Mac, go to the Edit drop-down in your browser and choose Emoji & Symbols. You will then be able to click on the symbol you want and insert. Simple!

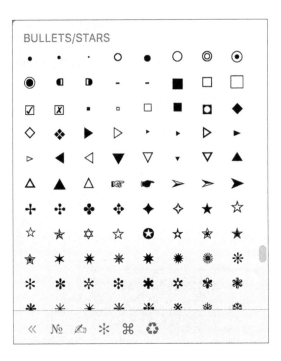

Want to see what some graphically designed profiles look like? See The Essay Expert's Sample LinkedIn Profiles.[51]

> **Note:** When you create a .pdf of your profile, these creative bullets appear as # signs. In my opinion, this slight glitch is worth it for the style it gives your on-line profile.

> **Here's another quick tip:** The "pipe" (|) is a useful formatting tool. You can copy this character as well from my profile, or find the character on your keyboard (it's usually on the same key as the backslash \ ). The pipe is most useful in your headline, e.g., Executive Resume Writer | C-Level Resumes | Board Resumes. It's clean and efficient.

Here's an example of a profile that utilizes this graphic successfully:

Vice President, Global Product Quality & Engineering PMO

Coupa Software

Jan 2014 – Nov 2016 • 2 yrs 11 mos • San Francisco Bay Area

A leader in the SaaS spend management solution development space brought me in to manage daily operations of Global Quality Engineering and the Engineering Program Management Office (PMO). I was asked to drive a few core objectives, including:

▶ Scaling the test engineering team and capabilities to meet Coupa's rapid growth objectives
▶ Expanding test coverage and test program effectiveness
▶ Improving the process for defect resolution
▶ Creating a direct communication pipeline with our customers

I built a comprehensive vision and roadmap for achieving these goals. My team and I embarked on a journey to make them happen and go well beyond the original business expectations in just an 18-month time frame.

ENGINEERING TRANSFORMATION & AUTOMATION
✓ Converted an almost all-manual testing process into a fully automated testing framework
✓ 15x increase in test automation coverage
✓ Eliminated multiple regression cycles
✓ Cut test case run time from 8 hours for 200 test cases to 20 minutes for 8,000 test cases
✓ Created a defect resolution framework that continuously analyzed test coverage, customer scenarios, and root causes

STRATEGY EXECUTION
✓ Designed and executed a strategy to update our SaaS product suite and seamlessly transition all customers to the same version

TEAM DEVELOPMENT
✓ Grew the QE team from 10 to an 45-person organization

Results to Expect

Your profile will have a professional, clean and attractive look, and you'll be creating a brand with your graphic presentation. People will enjoy the experience of reading your profile, compliment you, and maybe even copy some of your ideas (the sincerest form of flattery!)

Mistake #12

Blank or Skimpy Skills & Endorsements Sections

The Problem

The Skills & Endorsements section is your best opportunity to appear in recruiters' searches conducted for people with your skills.

Many people don't take the Skills & Endorsements section seriously because anyone can endorse you for a skill, even if they don't have first-hand experience of your skill level. Nevertheless, recruiters do use this feature, so if you do not complete the Skills section, you will lose leverage in your job search.

The Tune-Up

You'll need to complete a few other steps in setting up your profile before LinkedIn will allow you to add skills, such as your location, current position, education, industry, and profile photo. Once you've achieved Intermediate Level, you'll see a button to "Add a profile section." Select "Skills" from the drop-down:

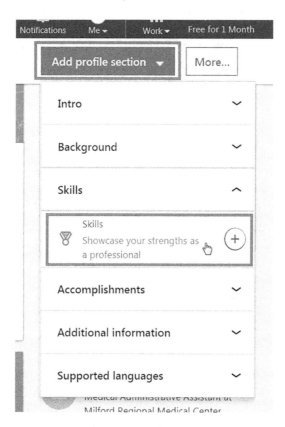

LinkedIn will suggest some skills for you based on the content of your profile:

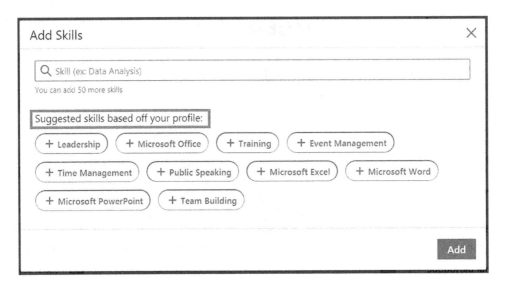

You can select the skills that apply to you (or you can add other skills, but I don't recommend that, as explained below).

Begin typing your desired skill and you will be given a list to choose from; whenever possible, choose skills that auto-populate, since these are the skills most searched for, especially by recruiters. You can add up to 50 skills.

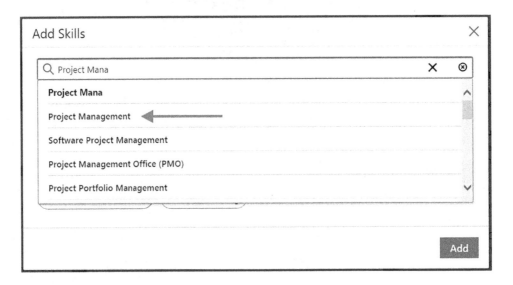

You can remove skills, too, or to a certain extent, rearrange them. To remove a skill, simply click the trash can icon next to its name.

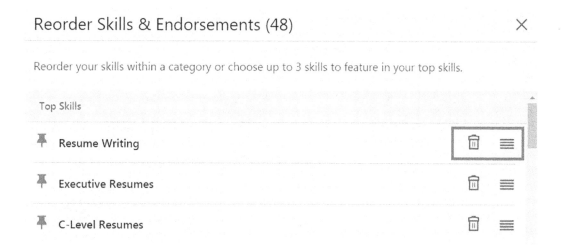

To rearrange your skills, grab the four lines to the right of the skill and drag and drop it to the correct spot so that your most pertinent skills are located at the top of the list. Save to complete your changes. Unfortunately, you can't control what category your skills show up in. LinkedIn will divide your skills into the categories Industry Knowledge, Tools & Technologies, Interpersonal Skills, and Other Skills—and there's nothing you can do about the order of these sections, nor about where each skill appears.

Managing Those Crazy Endorsements

Skills & Endorsements

To show or hide individual endorsements, click on the number of connections next to that skill.

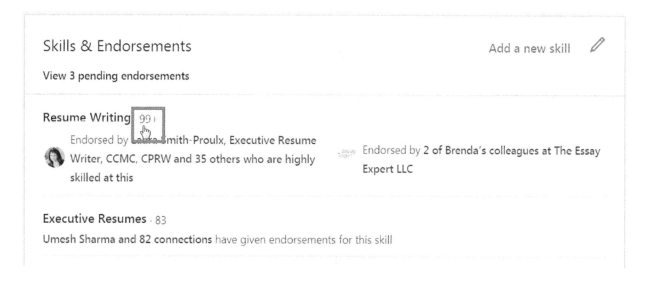

You'll then see a list of Endorsers. Click the switch to turn the endorsement from that connection off for that skill.

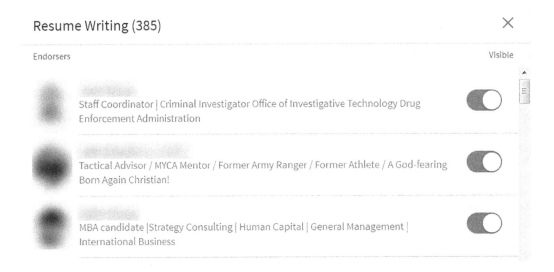

The Gift of Giving

If you're not getting as many endorsements as you'd like, try endorsing other people! You might be amazed at how quickly they return the favor.

Endorsing others can put you top of mind. Here's how:

If you come across a connection you'd like to endorse, click on their photo to be taken to their profile and scroll down to their Skills & Endorsements section. Next to each skill, you'll see a plus sign (if you've already endorsed them, it will be a check mark). Click the plus next to each skill you'd like to endorse and you're done. The connection will then receive an email letting them know you've endorsed them.

Via mobile, connections' top skills will be listed for you as their "featured" skills. You can endorse them for one of these or click to see more skills.

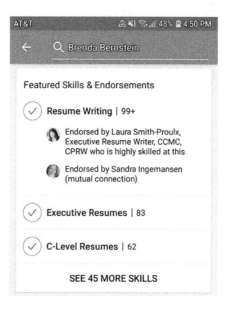

Also, LinkedIn's mobile app will also suggest endorsements more specifically based on how you know that person. For instance, if you both worked at a company that specializes in personal branding, LinkedIn will ask if you'd like to endorse that person for that particular skill.

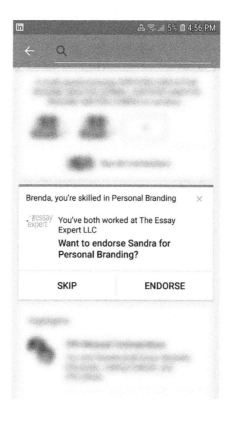

And if you had previously endorsed someone for a skill, you may be asked to provide a skill level.

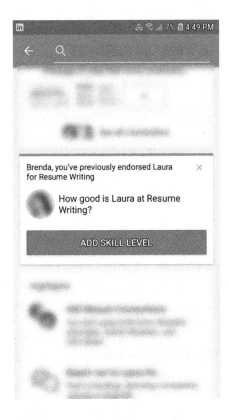

You have control over whether LinkedIn suggests endorsements for you to your connections, and over whether you receive endorsement suggestions from your connections. To edit your settings, click on the pencil icon:

. At the bottom of the next window, click on "Adjust endorsements settings."

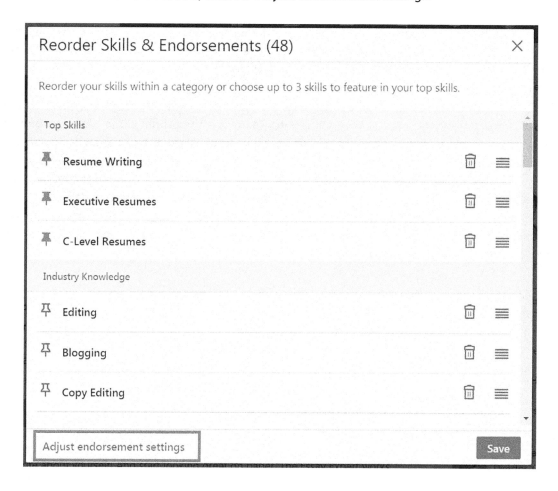

Here's an article from the LinkedIn® Blog about Endorsements[52] that provides some solid advice about giving and receiving endorsements. I recommend that you read it!

Results to Expect

LinkedIn states that "accumulating a high number of endorsements for a skill adds credibility to your profile, and shows that your professional network recognizes you have that skill," as well as "contributes to the strength of [your] profile, and increases the likelihood [you'll] be discovered for opportunities related to the skills [your] connections know [you] possess."

More endorsements and more traffic to your profile mean more opportunities for you. According to Link Humans, "members who include skills get around 13 times more profile views." And LinkedIn states that members with more than 5 skills are 27x more likely to be discovered in searches by recruiters. Furthermore, people will understand better where your skills lie; they will endorse you, giving you more credibility; and recruiters will *find* you when they search on your skills. The more endorsements you have as a job seeker, the more likely you are to be contacted by a recruiter with a premium account.

If you can get 99+ endorsements for any skill, it will be hard for potential clients and employers not to give you some credit. In contrast, having few endorsements for a skill can be a bad sign. So as long as endorsements are part of your LinkedIn profile, take them seriously.

Mistake #13

Not Staying Active through Activity Updates, Publishing, Comments and Kudos

The Problem

There are multiple ways to stay active on LinkedIn. More and more, your activity level plays a big role in how well you perform in searches. If you don't post valuable information, conduct relevant searches, and participate in conversations, you won't be seen as an attractive candidate by recruiters—and you could be seen as a net taker (vs. a net giver) on LinkedIn.

The Tune-Up

The Share bar, which can be accessed from your homepage, is a good place to start when sharing information on LinkedIn. You might be familiar with this type of function if you spend time on Twitter or Facebook. Here's what it looks like:

This feature is your opportunity to let your readers know that you're active in your life and in your field. If you do not use this function, your name and updates will not appear in the ongoing activity feed found on your connections' homepages.

It's essential on LinkedIn to keep your updates current and to share valuable information consistently. Use hash tags to get your content in front of those searching for specific topics.

Don't stop at posting yourself. Read and comment on other peoples' articles. Write articles yourself! And explore the many tools available to help you collect and curate great information for sharing. Here are just a few:

- **Pocket:**[53] Save articles, blog posts, videos and images for later use.
- **Feedly:**[54] Follow blogs, podcasts, YouTube channels and publications, and access the content anytime.
- **Google Alerts:**[55] Get email notifications when Google finds new results on a topic that interests you.
- **Listly:**[56] Create lists of just about anything and let people contribute.

Once you know what's important for you to share and what articles you want to interact with, you have many ways to do so. Six good options are highlighted below:

Option #1: Share Updates Directly from Your LinkedIn Home Page

After accessing your Sharing bar from the Home tab, write something current—about what you're learning, a project you're working on, even your latest favorite quotation. Show us you're alive! You might even choose to reveal your sense of humor (keep it clean folks!) Some clients have had success posting that they are seeking to relocate to a particular city—it is possible to catch the attention of recruiters that way.

You can include articles, photos, presentations, or videos with your updates. To share an image, for example, click the "Image" button and choose a photo from your files.

This is what your post will look like:

Don't forget to add "alt text" to your images—text that describes what's in the images. Alt text allows search engines to index the pictures you share, so be sure to include keywords to help you get found. Just click "Add alt text" and include a description.

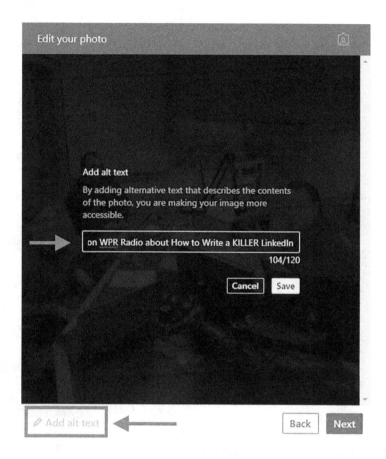

Your alt text will be visible if for any reason your image does not appear. This allows readers to understand what your photo was about even if they are not able to view it. Note that adding alt text is not available in the mobile app yet, as of April 2019.

Photo Tagging

If a LinkedIn connection appears in your photo, tag them! After selecting your image, click on the member you want to identify and a search field will appear. Begin typing in the name of your connection, then click their profile to tag them.

Tagged connections will be notified of your post and also have the ability to remove the tag if they wish.

There is some concern that spammers will use tagging to harass LinkedIn users. Only time will tell.

Video on LinkedIn – Now with Stickers!

If you really want to get attention, share a video. You can either paste your video URL, or if you want to share a file directly from your computer, click on "Video":

Videos posted from your computer will look something like this:

With LinkedIn's mobile app, you can add text and stickers to your videos and images.

There doesn't currently seem to be a way to search the available stickers, so you'll need to scroll through them to find one you like. Perhaps LinkedIn will improve that functionality in the future, as well as increase the limited number of options available.

Mentions: Give Credit Where Credit is Due

LinkedIn's "Mentions" feature is a great little tool for crediting connections in your updates—or to simply include people and let them know you're thinking about them and want them to pay attention. If you type the "@" symbol, followed by the name of a connection or a company in your Update box or a comment field on the homepage, the field will auto-generate potential people or companies you can mention. (*For more information, see this LinkedIn Help article.*[57])

To mention a connection, start typing the person's name and select the correct name from the drop-down. Then write your post and click the Share button. The person or company you mentioned will automatically be notified.

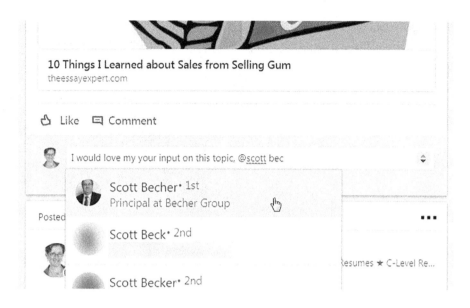

If you get mentioned and you don't want the publicity, you can remove the mention (see Removing a Mention of Yourself[58]). You can also control your settings to prevent mentions.[59]

In addition to first-degree connections, you can mention those LinkedIn members who are engaged in conversations about posts. This means you can essentially start conversations with people even if they are not in your network. You can also respond in real time in the comments section of a post when someone—even someone not in your network—initiates a conversation there with you.

Option #2: Use HootSuite

HootSuite.com allows you to send updates to Facebook and LinkedIn all with one click. You can simply post the update you want to HootSuite and schedule it to post to the social media site you choose at the time you choose. Or if you have your own blog or a favorite blog by someone else, you can send an RSS feed (a stream that contains each of the articles as it is posted) to the social media account(s) of your choosing. That way your blog posts can automatically post to your LinkedIn Activity Update bar.

Here's how to share your blog:

After logging in to HootSuite, hover over your profile photo on the right upper corner of your account. Click on Account & Settings:

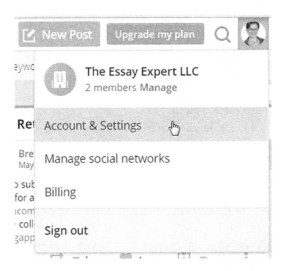

Select the RSS/Atom menu and click the "+" sign to add a new feed. You will need to upgrade to a paid account ($5.99/month) to use this feature.

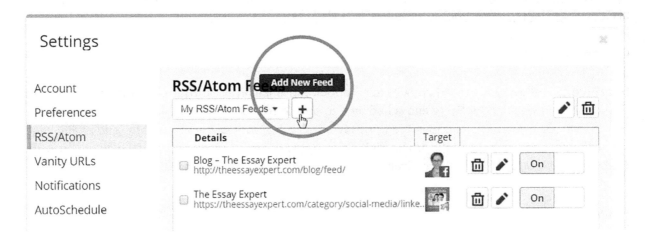

Paste your feed URL in the field provided. Then select the social sites you would like the feed to post to.

Edit any other preferred options and Save Feed.

For posting WordPress blogs to your LinkedIn profile or other social media accounts, you can also use the *Publicize* function from the JetPack Plugin.[60]

Option #3: Publish Articles

According to LinkedIn's Official Blog post, The Definitive Professional Publishing Platform:[61]

> "When a member publishes a [long-form] post on LinkedIn, their original content becomes part of their professional profile, is shared with their trusted network and [can] reach the largest group of professionals ever assembled. Now members have the ability to follow other members that are not in their network and build their own group of followers."

LinkedIn's total publishing platform includes: 1) sharing updates via your homepage and 2) publishing long-form posts, or articles. Both are accessed from the same place on your homepage. Perhaps the coolest thing about these long-form posts is that they are searchable *outside* of LinkedIn. That means readers don't even need to have a LinkedIn account in order to view your work. Your articles will show up in Google searches!! Think of the reach you can have.

Are you concerned about copyright on the articles you publish on LinkedIn? Here's a message from LinkedIn regarding published content:

> At LinkedIn, we want to help you make the most of your professional life. Part of that is showing the world more about who you are and what you know by sharing ideas, starting conversations, and inspiring others with your work.
>
> So, that raises a question: who owns all of the content you post on LinkedIn? You do, and you always have. We've updated our User Agreement[62] (effective October 23, 2014) to reinforce our commitment to respecting what's yours. Whether it's an update, photo, comment, post, presentation, portfolio, or anything else, we want to make it clear that you're in control of your content.
>
> Here are some highlights:
>
> - **You're in the driver's seat.** We'll always ask your permission before using your content in third-party ads, publications, or websites. We've always done this, but now our User Agreement specifically spells it out.
>
> - **You decide when your content goes.** If you delete something from our platform, we won't use it anymore.
>
> - **Share wherever or whenever you'd like.** We don't own or have exclusive rights to your content. It's yours, so feel free to repost it anywhere, however you want.
>
> Thanks for being a member!
> The LinkedIn Team

All members of English-speaking countries have the ability to publish long-form posts; and LinkedIn plans to expand that privilege to all of the languages they support.

To create a long-form post, go to your homepage and click on "Write an article":

You will arrive at a page where you can create a new post. To publish an article, insert your content, along with images and pertinent links.

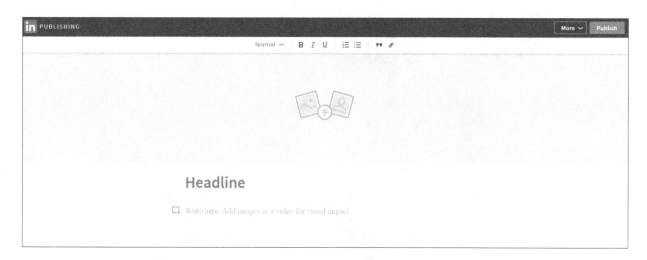

Over 40,000 articles are published every week. According to a study by OkDork and Search Wilderness,[63] the most successful posts followed these guidelines:

1. Keep your title short and sweet. Titles with more than 40-49 characters can get cut off.
2. Make it visual. Posts with at least 8 images perform 2.4 times better.
3. Don't use videos and other multimedia! This might be surprising, but fewer people view articles that include videos (as opposed to static images, which boost views).
4. Instruct. "How-to" and list-style headlines performed better than headlines posed as a question.
5. Keep it clear. Include subheadings—ideally 5 of them—so your article is easy to read.
6. Maintain a reasonable length. Articles between 1900 and 2000 words are read more often.
7. Go neutral. Posts that were neither positive or negative ranked higher.
8. Simplify. Articles that met the reading level of an 11-year-old ranked better.
9. Promote. Share your LinkedIn publisher post on other social networks!
10. Get Likes. The more Likes you have, the more views you will get.

Always proofread your article before publishing!

Here is what your post will look like on the homepage of your connections:

Each time someone likes or comments on your post, it is brought to the top of the page again.

Your posts will appear in your "Articles & activity" section of your profile. They can be searched via the search bar as well.

Interested readers will click through to see your articles and other posts, where they can then follow you and comment on your activity. Social media statistics and share buttons above your post allow readers to spread your work beyond LinkedIn!

James Carbary suggests writing "long-form" status updates instead of publishing articles for more views. In his experience, LinkedIn gives more exposure to status updates than articles. I'm not sure if I agree, but if you want to try it, here's what he says: "Status updates have a limit of 1,300 characters (which is approximately 250-300 words). This means that you can spend much less time creating content that gets far greater reach. Make sure that the first sentence of your status update is captivating. People are scrolling their LinkedIn feed at lightning speed, and they'll only see the first one or two sentences of your post as they scroll."[64]

Your Articles on Social Media

Make sure to share your article with your social media networks, either by using a service like Hootsuite or by clicking the Share button.

One important tip, suggested by the Content Marketing Institute[65] and updated by Inc.[66], is to send a tweet to "tip @LinkedInEditors" with your post to improve the odds a LinkedIn editor will see it and it be published on LinkedIn Pulse.

Publishing articles will generate a wide audience and could turn you into a "top influencer" on LinkedIn if your posts are popular enough. Some of mine have been viewed by thousands of people. Sharing original content will also result in Google rankings for your articles on LinkedIn.

According to LinkedIn's Official Blog,[67] "When a LinkedIn member shares six pieces of content, on average, they receive six profile views and make two new connections, which helps them strengthen their professional brands. At the same time, the company they work for receives six job views, three Company Page views, and one Company Page follower, which helps them better hire, market, and sell."

Every time you post original content, you establish yourself further as a thought leader in your field.

Who's Viewing Your Articles?

To find out whose eyes are on your articles, scroll down to the "Your Dashboard" section of your profile and click on the "Article views" link.

Your Dashboard		
Private to you		☆ All Star
973	220	298
Who viewed your profile	Article views	Search appearances

You'll be brought to a feed of your articles:

Click on the " . . . views" link at the bottom and you'll discover what portion of your readers are from certain areas, demographics and networks. If someone you want to connect with has viewed your article, it's a great foundation from which to reach out and send an invitation.

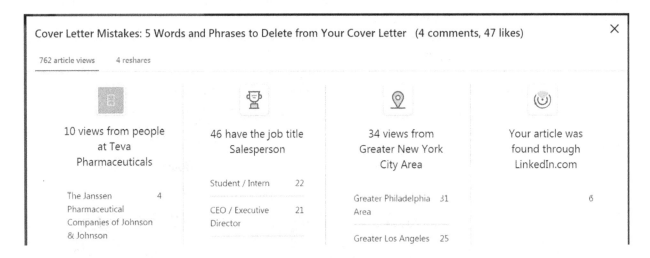

Leveraging SEO for your published articles

Be sure to utilize keywords in your posted articles. LinkedIn uses a special algorithm to tag long-form posts into categories called "channels" and to suggest posts for its members. If your article is tagged, it will appear to LinkedIn members with the most relevant profile content. So do some keyword research for your field, or hire someone to do it for you, and build your posts using SEO practices! This strategy will help you in Google search results too.

For LinkedIn's tips and best practices for publishing articles, visit LinkedIn's Help Center topic Publishing Articles on LinkedIn – Overview.[68]

Have you utilized LinkedIn's article publishing feature? If so, what benefits have you enjoyed? And if not, what are you waiting for?

Option #4: Share Across LinkedIn

Share other people's updates from the items that appear on your homepage. To do this, look at the bottom of the update you wish to share and click on Share:

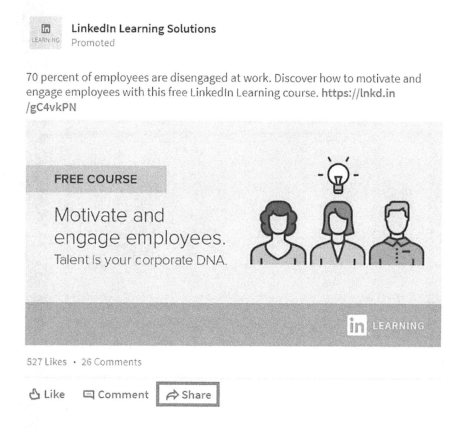

You will have the option to share with everyone (Public), anyone on LinkedIn and Twitter, or just your network (Connections). You can also share with individuals and include a personalized message simultaneously.

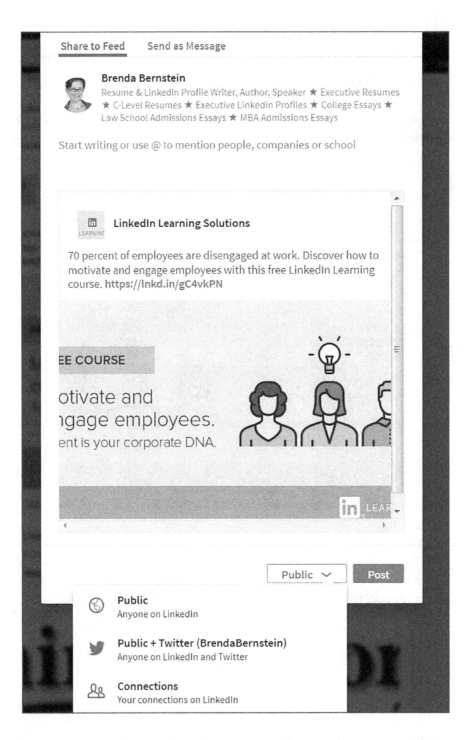

Sharing other people's posts is a great way to encourage them to share yours. Helping each other out is a primary tenet of networking, and this is an easy way to do it!

Tip: According to Entrepreneur article, "How to Get Thousands of Views on Your LinkedIn Content,"[69] you can garner more clicks by not including a link in your status updates—put a link in the first comment instead. In testing this theory, author James Carbary "went from getting 100-200 views per post to getting over 5,000 views per post."

Customizing Your Feed

You can select what you want to see in your Homepage feed. This feature is designed to help you find content more easily and to control the type of information that comes through your LinkedIn feed, making it easier to read and share relevant news and articles.
Learn how to edit your feed preferences in **Appendix H**.

Finding Shareable Content via Mobile – and Controlling Your Feed

In October, 2016, LinkedIn kindly outlined[70] the three newest features available to you via your mobile phone.

a. Customizable Feed

Click the three dots (or down arrow) in the upper right corner of your mobile app to reveal the "Improve my feed" option. Pick topics that interest you, follow leaders you want to hear from, and tap on publications you like to read. Also, you can unfollow or hide updates from connections that you find less interesting, and the app will deliver more of what you like to read and share.

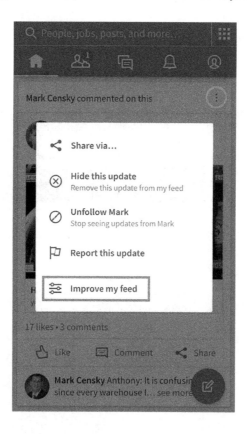

b. Save Content for Later

iOS: At the bottom right of each article, there is now an option to bookmark it so you can come back to it later.

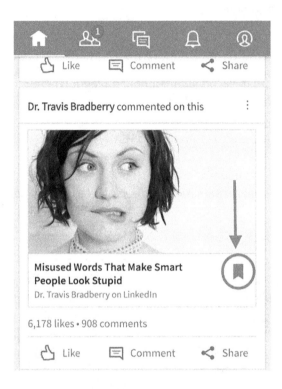

To access your saved content, click on your profile image.

Then scroll down to the "Your Dashboard" section:

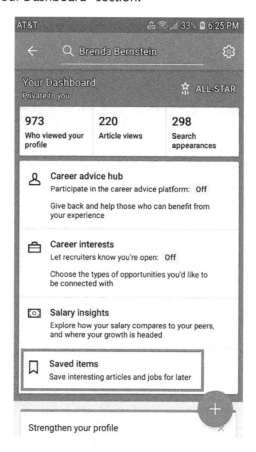

Android: To save an article, click the down arrow next to the article title:

Then select "Save article" from the drop-down menu.

Accessing saved articles works the same way on all mobile devices.

c. Search for Content

The mobile app's search box allows you to find the content that interests you most.

In addition to these three, LinkedIn has also created Trending Storylines,[71] which displays items "personalized for you by a combination of algorithms" at the top of your profile:

Want tips on how to hide posts and unfollow people or companies? Check out LinkedIn's Official Blog article, Simple Tips to Improve your LinkedIn Feed.[72]

Option #5: Give Kudos

As of June 2018, LinkedIn began rolling out "Kudos" for their mobile app. This tool gives you the ability in a post to dole out a quick pat on the back to your connections. Doing this will keep you top of mind with your contacts and possibly help you in your LinkedIn search rankings, as the more active you are on LinkedIn, the better for you in LinkedIn's algorithm.

To give Kudos, click the plus icon at the bottom of your home page to begin a post.

Choose Give Kudos from the bottom of your draft window.

Then search for the person you want to give the kudos to, check the circle to the right of their name, and click Next.

LinkedIn will offer images to accompany your post, similar to a greeting card, and include accolades for being a team player, an inspirational leader, and more. You can even send a simple thank you.

Your post should mention the name of your connection (see how to use the @mention feature above) and why you are praising them.

Your connection will see your post in their Mentions.

And your post will look something like this:

Kudos can also be accessed from your connection's profile page by the "More" button below their Headline.

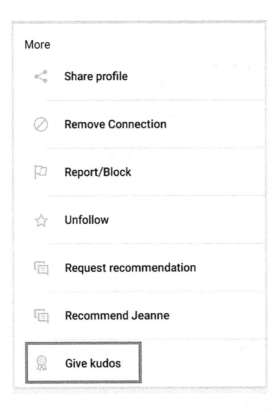

Using kudos to boast about your coworkers can show the world that you're a team player. If you own a business, this is also an excellent opportunity to acknowledge your employees or thank a colleague and build your social brand at the same time.

Option #6: Comment and React

Stay active on LinkedIn. When you add a connection, add or comment on a group conversation, post a job, or even just like another Update, it will go into LinkedIn's news feed and show up on your connections' homepages.

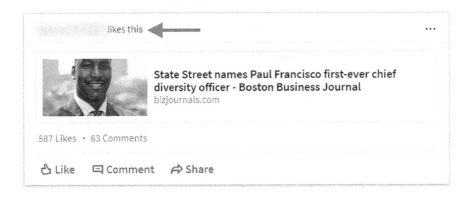

As of April 11, 2019, LinkedIn is rolling out "reaction." Much like on Facebook, members will now be able to not only like a post, but also, love it, celebrate it, tag it as insightful or express their curiosity.

If these new reaction images are not enough, you can include your own images with your comments to really stand out. You can share an event photo, a screenshot of an article with relevant content highlighted, infographics, and more.

An image can draw more attention to your comment, so go for it! Click on the camera icon and attach any photo from your files. Note that you can't post an image only; you must also leave a written comment.

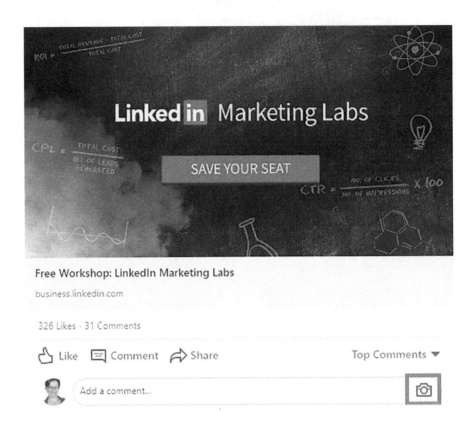

Free Workshop: LinkedIn Marketing Labs

business.linkedin.com

326 Likes · 31 Comments

Like   Comment   Share   Top Comments ▼

Add a comment...

Here's what your image might look like in a conversation:

GIFs

You can also add GIFs and emojis. While I understand that GIFs can be cute, funny, weird, and many other things, I don't think they belong on a business platform. However, if you want to use GIFs in more casual interactions on LinkedIn, have fun! Just click the GIF option below your message and type in a search term.

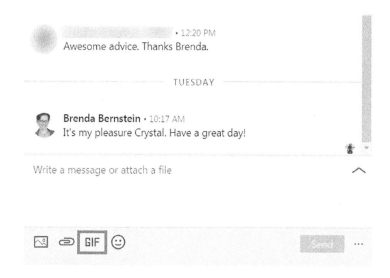

For more details on using LinkedIn GIFs, read LinkedIn Official Blog's article "Make Conversations More Engaging with GIFs in Messaging."[73]

Emojis

You can now use colorful characters in your Headline, as well as in most sections and titles in your LinkedIn profile. If you want to add some visual appeal, an appropriate emoji can be a bold addition.

> ☀ Our Commitment
> At The Essay Expert, we don't go to bed until we know we've captured your essence. That's what gets each one of us up in the morning, because that's what will excite the right company about you. Not the person next to you. Not a list of bullet points. You.
>
> ☀ Our philosophy: Listen for greatness. Produce outstanding work, on time, every time.
>
> ☀ Our values: ★ Personal Attention ★ Reliability ★ Responsiveness ★ Integrity ★ Service ★ Trust ★ Partnership ★ Creativity ★ Contribution ★ Excellence

Note that not all symbols will render in color once you've updated, so you may need to experiment. Also, this function might not work on all computers or browsers, so some viewers may see an empty box instead of the symbol you chose. I would personally recommend sticking to Unicode characters to be safe (See **Mistake #10** for more on using unicode characters). Have fun!

A Note on Privacy

Do you want your activity history to be viewable to the public? You have a choice. Go to your Settings & Privacy, click on the Privacy tab, and under "Blocking and hiding," click "Followers":

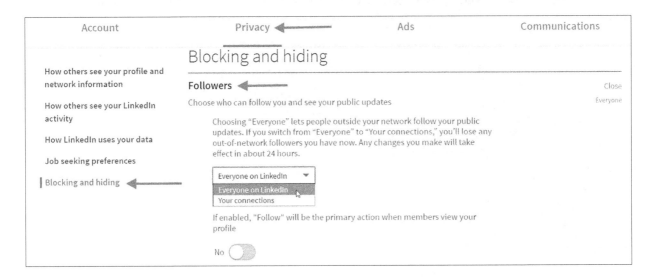

Everyone has different considerations when choosing how public to be with their profile, so choose the option that meets your needs and goals.

You also have control over whether you want your connections to be notified when you are mentioned in a post with the @Mention feature:

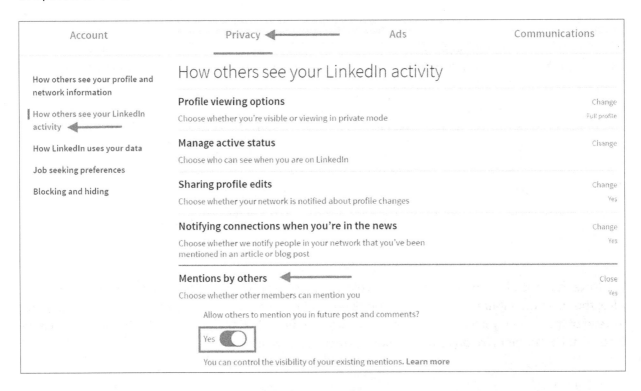

Option #7: Interact with Company Pages

If you are a job seeker or if you are a vendor wanting to work with a particular company, it's more and more important to follow the company on LinkedIn and to interact with the company's talent brand. Recruiters are watching for this! So do your homework and show your interest by engaging with the company. You will make a big impact by showing up and participating in the company's conversations.

Here's an example of what that might look like:

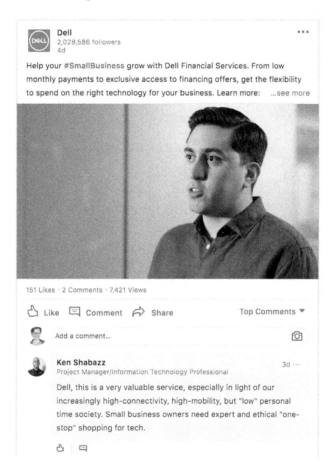

Note: Only follow companies that are respectable and match up with your brand. Unfollow any others that could make you look unfocused. Following irrelevant companies could be a negative to recruiters checking you out.

Results to Expect

LinkedIn reaches more followers per post (20%) than Facebook (2%) or Twitter (4%)! So be sure to put this tool to good use.

The more you post updates and share them, and the more you interact with the content on LinkedIn, the more your activity will be publicized and the more you will stay top of mind with your connections and recruiters. If you play your cards right, you could very well start to be seen as an expert in your field.

If you've built your network to 1000+, you'll have more leverage when you post, as there will be more people who are likely to share your posts with their connections. This positive activity will attract the attention of recruiters and potential clients who want to know how you are participating and sharing on LinkedIn.

If my own experience is any indication, the more active you are in sharing information, the more you will be noticed by potential clients and employers; many of the people who read and engage with your offerings will remember you and tell their connections about you. In a business world where networking is king, you can't ask for better than that.

Mistake #14

Special Sections not Utilized

The Problem

Special Sections: LinkedIn frequently adds new sections appropriate for special groups like artists and students, for activities like volunteerism, and for skills like languages. You might fall into one of these categories and be at a disadvantage to the scientist who completed a Patents section; the student who completed the Courses section; or the civic-minded professional with a robust Volunteer Experience section. Furthermore, you might be at a loss when attempting to include all the aspects of who you are into your profile unless you utilize some of these special sections.

The Tune-Up

These sections allow you to present information in an organized fashion so you don't have to get everything across in your Summary or Experience sections. If you are an artist, use the Portfolio section. If you have taken courses you want to report, check out the Courses section. Speak languages? Try Languages. Volunteer? Complete the Volunteer section! And according to LinkedIn, 42% of hiring managers said they consider volunteer experience equal to formal work experience.[74] You don't have to fit it all into the Experience section!

    Other sections include Publications, Courses, Languages, Projects, Honors & Awards, Organizations, Test Scores, Certifications and Patents. You can even post your blog under your Publications section; just add a live URL that links directly to your blog for anyone who wants to take a look.

Here's what some of the sections look like:

4 Honors & Awards   ∧

Certified Master Resume Writer (CMRW)
Feb 2013 • Career Directors International

This Master-Level certification, the pinnacle level of competency for CDI, required Brenda to demonstrate her superior knowledge and experience in contemporary resume writing through an intensive examination of her professional writing. She was assessed on her broad range of industry knowledge and expertise in the areas of strategy, branding, advanced visual appeal, and contextual narrative. Recognition as a CMRW sets Ms. Bernstein apart from the competition and distinguishes the high caliber of her credentials in assisting clientele with professional resume services.

TORI Award Winner, Best New Graduate Resume, 3rd Place
Oct 2012 • Career Directors International

Each year, CDI hosts the resume writing industry's most prestigious Toast of the Resume Industry™ (TORI) resume writing competition. This is an international competition in which contestants submit their best work in a category.

4 Publications   ∧

How to Write a STELLAR Executive Resume: 50 Tips to Reach Your Job Search Target
Sep 2013 • The Essay Expert

As an executive conducting a job search, you might never have had to write a resume before, and you might be feeling unsure of where to start. This book provides an easy-to-read, practical and up-to-date guide on best practices in writing your Executive Resume. How to Write a STELLAR Executive Resume takes you through the resume writing process step by step, from thinking through your approach to creating a professional format, crafting effective branding statements and bullets, and handling specific challenges.

Whether you are a resume writer catering to executives or a senior-level job seeker, you will learn valuable tips from How to Write a STELLAR Executive Resume!

See publication

To add a section, click on the "Add profile section" in the upper right.

Add profile section ▼   More...

Then click the desired section to add it to your profile.

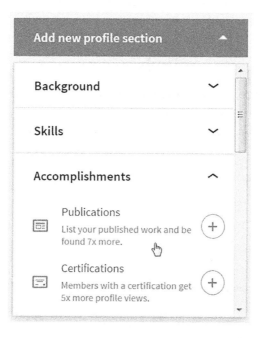

A pop-up window will appear and you can begin adding your information.

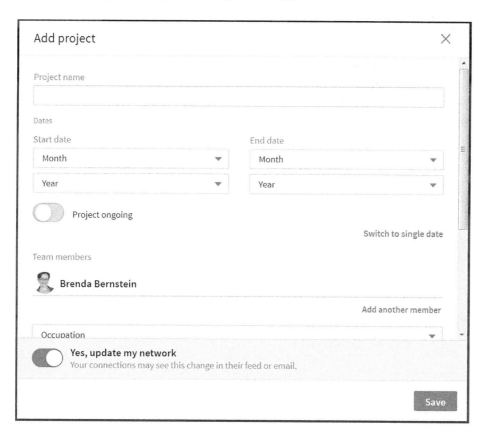

As with any profile changes, you can choose to share your additions with your connections or keep them private by toggling the "update my network" button.

You can get creative with what you list where. For instance, list your blog as a publication and include the link, allowing people to click directly to the blog. Or list details of projects in the Projects section that you don't have room to explain in your Summary or Experience sections. For courses associated with a degree, use the Education section.

Entries within the Experience, Volunteer & Education sections can be reordered. Just grab the four black bars to the right of the entry to drag and drop them. These bars will appear when you hover over the position (if there are no black bars present, the entry cannot be moved).

Results to Expect

By adding special sections, you will be able to share much more information than would otherwise be possible; and you can organize it in a way that brings attention to important aspects of your career and education. No longer will you struggle with how to share about your volunteerism, impressive courses or accomplishments. It's all laid out neatly for you!

Mistake #15

No Media Items in your Summary and Experience Sections

The Problem

LinkedIn's media attachment function allows users to add links to images, presentations, videos, and documents to their profiles.

If you don't use this function, your profile will be one-dimensional (i.e., boring) and you will miss out on accessible, free marketing for yourself and your business.

The Tune-Up

In your Summary and Experience sections, you can add files or links to videos, images, documents or presentations by clicking on the pencil icon next to your profile image.

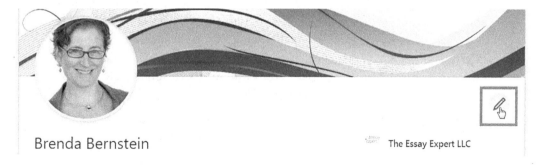

Scroll down to your Summary and you will see the following:

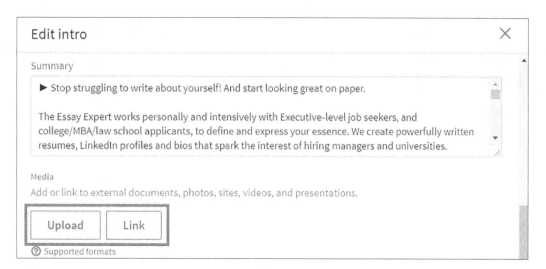

The possibilities are endless of what you can link to or upload here. If you choose "Upload" you will be brought to your computer's document files.

Following are some ideas of material you can use to populate the Portfolio function on your LinkedIn profile; some of these ideas come from the days of Partner Applications!

I. Events

If you are promoting an event, attach the link so you can include an event image right in your Summary or Experience section.

II. Documents, including your Resume

Here's what my multi-media portfolio looks like with a resume uploaded directly to the profile:

Show more ⌄

> **Note:** If you choose to post your resume to LinkedIn, you may want to remove your address from the header. Assuming you have a public profile, your resume, along with the information on it, will be available to the public. Unfortunately, it will also be available to hackers if they break into LinkedIn, which we know is a real possibility from the events of June 6, 2012 (when multiple LinkedIn profiles were hacked).
>
> What do you want to share with your LinkedIn audience? You can build your image through adding links to any important documents and web pages. Have fun!

III. LinkedIn SlideShare

You can log in to LinkedIn SlideShare with your LinkedIn username and password and import your LinkedIn profile information to complete your SlideShare profile. With a single click, you can follow all your LinkedIn contacts through SlideShare, thus ensuring that you receive notifications of their updated content and comments. You can also announce your SlideShare uploads to your connections.

To get your new presentation to show up as an update in all of your connections' homepage feeds, first make sure to switch the "Sharing profile edits" option in your Settings & Privacy to on:

You can easily access SlideShare from your LinkedIn profile by clicking on the Work drop-down:

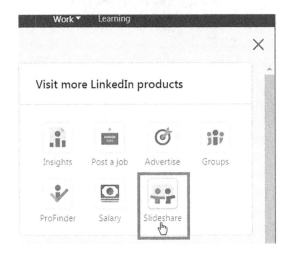

To post a SlideShare presentation to your Summary section automatically, go to your list of presentations by hovering over your profile image and clicking "My uploads":

Hovering over the image of your presentation will reveal a pop-up button to add that presentation to your profile.

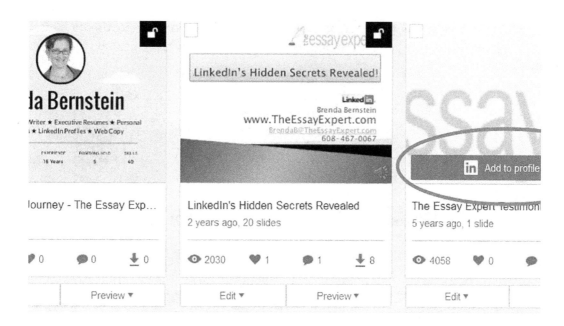

If you are logged into SlideShare with LinkedIn, clicking the Add to Profile button will automatically add your presentation to your Summary and share it with your connections. Here is how the announcement will appear:

If you would like to add your presentation to your Experience section instead, use the presentation's direct link or URL. To find the link, open your presentation by clicking on its image, then grab the URL from your browser's search bar.

Next, go to your profile and the position you'd like to add the presentation to, then click on the pencil icon:

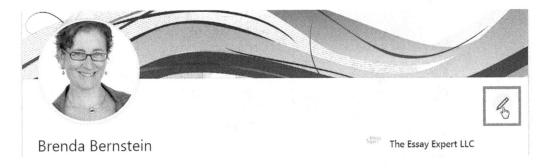

Clicking on the "Link" button will reveal a field where you can paste in the file URL. Click "Add," then enter your presentation title and description.

The presentation or video will then be part of your LinkedIn profile until you decide to remove or change it, plus your connections will be notified via their homepage feed that you have added it.

Note that SlideShare also has a useful Clipping tool that allows you to isolate specific slides containing the information you'd most like to share.

When someone clips one of your slides, SlideShare will notify you so you can see what your viewers are most interested in.

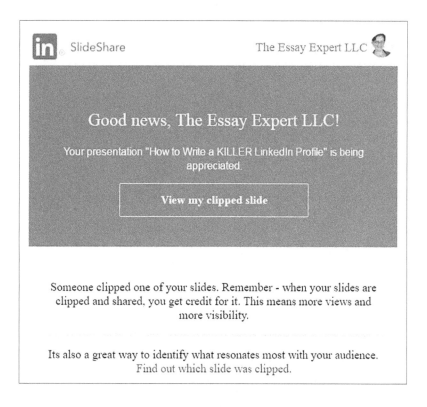

For more about the Clipping feature, read LinkedIn's help article, Using the Clipping Feature on Slideshare.[75] As reported by Forbes,[76] "More than 80% of traffic to SlideShare currently comes from search, and Clipping should make it easier to discover slides through other sources, according to LinkedIn's Caroline Gaffney, who leads SlideShare's product team. SlideShare has about 70 million monthly active users, and content on the platform has nearly doubled since 2013."

For more on LinkedIn SlideShare, view the LinkedIn Help article SlideShare - Frequently Asked Questions.[77]

Results to Expect

Your profile will be a multi-media event! Readers will have fun scrolling through your profile and be impressed that you utilized LinkedIn's technology to its full advantage.

By sharing your events, relevant reading, presentations, videos, documents, and resume in your Portfolio, you will remain a current and savvy LinkedIn user who attracts attention to your profile. A well-utilized Portfolio can lead to interest from both employers and customers who click on your links.

SECTION 3

Playing the LinkedIn Game to Win

Having a KILLER LinkedIn Profile is just the beginning. You then need to use it!

You could sit there with a keyword-optimized profile hoping for recruiters to contact you, and someday they might do that . . .

You could fly solo, not joining or participating in groups . . .

You could laze around and hope your contacts are inspired to recommend you . . .

You could write your profile and let it idle there for years, thinking you've fulfilled your LinkedIn duty . . .

You could do all those things, and maybe someone would contact you. But it's unlikely.

Instead, be proactive in using LinkedIn's Jobs functions and reaching out to your networking contacts. Join groups and leverage opportunities to share, learn and connect. Risk asking your connections to endorse and recommend you.

Your LinkedIn profile is a living, breathing creation that requires attention and care. This section shows you how to treat it that way so you experience KILLER results from your LinkedIn presence!

Mistake #16

Not Utilizing LinkedIn's Jobs Functions

The Problem

Whether you are a job seeker or an employer, you need to know about LinkedIn® Jobs. Jobs are so important on LinkedIn, in fact, that they have their own tab right in the top menu. The LinkedIn mobile app allows job seekers to apply for jobs using LinkedIn right from their phones.

LinkedIn's partnerships with the data-driven matching technology company Bright,[78] leading online learning company Lynda, and job search site, Snagajob,[79] are making LinkedIn increasingly powerful as a center for connecting talent with opportunity. The potential to streamline the candidate training and locating process is immense. LinkedIn also offers "Learning,"[80] a service that helps candidates secure better jobs by connecting them with live training programs from Lynda.com.

LinkedIn is becoming the #1 resource for job listings on the web and if you're not on this bandwagon it's time to jump on!

The Tune-Up for Job Seekers

Start exploring by clicking on "Jobs" in the top menu.

Your first consideration when actively looking for a new position on LinkedIn is whether you would like to keep your job search confidential. LinkedIn's "Open Candidates"[81] tool allows you to signal privately to recruiters that you are open to new job opportunities, though a recruiter could potentially tip off your company that you are looking—so be careful.

To turn this feature on, go to the Jobs menu, then under "Jobs you may be interested in," click on "Career interests." Toggle the "Let recruiters know you're open" switch to "On."

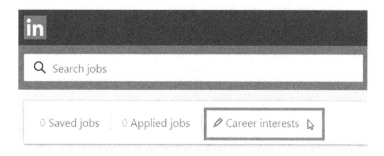

Want to speak directly to recruiters? Add a note in the bottom box to let them know the specifics of your job search.

LinkedIn will email you with helpful links to get you moving in the right direction.

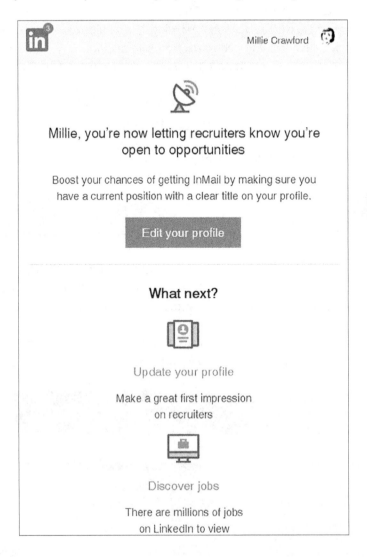

Open Candidates makes it easy to access hundreds of thousands of recruiters who are looking for talent on LinkedIn. It's available in the U.S., U.K. Canada and Australia on both the desktop and mobile versions of LinkedIn, and there are plans to roll out the program globally.

Conduct a Manual Job Search

In addition to the Open Candidates feature, you can also manually search for positions. Under the Jobs tab, you will automatically see a list of jobs that might interest you, based on the keywords in your profile.

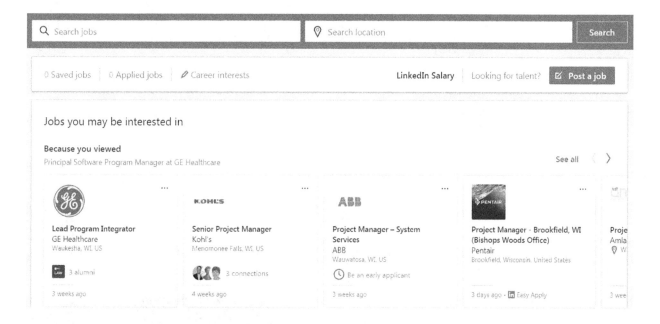

If you have a Premium account, you'll be greeted with a selection of jobs you would be a top applicant for. Other LinkedIn Premium features include company insights such as connections, teams you might work with, and growth and hiring trends. For more about job search features available with Premium, see LinkedIn's Premium Career[82] package options. I recommend that as a job seeker, you click on the Jobs tab daily. But don't stop there. Update your Preferences to search for the jobs you want in the geographic location that interests you. You can also expand your criteria by industry, skill level and company size. To access your preferences, click "Career Interests."

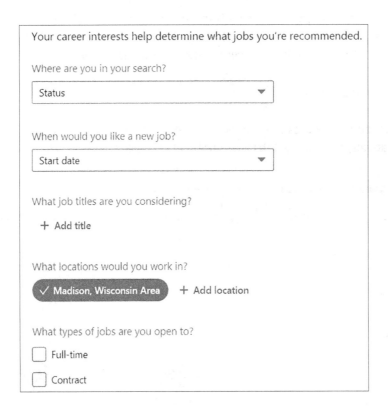

The search bar is another option for finding relevant jobs. When I searched for Account Executive Digital Media in Madison, WI, here's some of what came up:

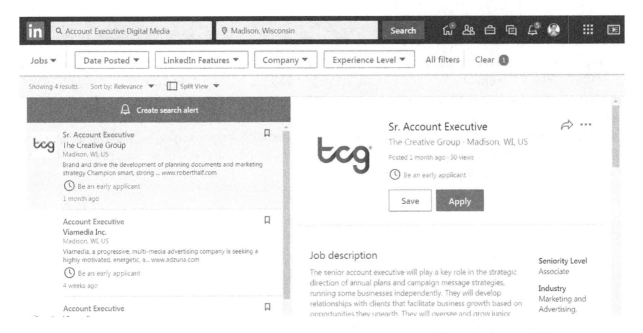

You can use Boolean logic to aid your search. Words such as not, and, and or can be used to include and exclude search variables. For more details on how to use this method, read LinkedIn Help's article, Using Boolean Search on LinkedIn.[83]

Once your search terms are entered, LinkedIn will provide a list of current positions which you can fine tune by location, company, date posted, job function, industry, experience level and title.

> **Important Caveat:** You want your searches and saved searches to be consistent with your skills, and consistent with each other. You will shoot yourself in the foot if you conduct searches for unrelated jobs because you will appear unfocused. So think through your job strategy on LinkedIn before starting your search!

Saving Searches

If you conduct a search you want to repeat regularly, click on "Create search alert" in the upper left-hand corner and you will be given an option to receive an alert daily or weekly for jobs that match your criteria. You can then conduct your saved search with one click from your Jobs page.

To receive job postings from your saved search in your inbox, select "Email." If you choose "Email & notifications," you will get notifications on LinkedIn and also through the LinkedIn app.

To receive push notifications about new job postings, make sure that option is on in your app's settings.

Wondering what happened to the LinkedIn Job Search app on your iOS or Android device? The app was discontinued as of May 2019. But never fear! All the functionality of the app is now available in your main LinkedIn app.

Mining LinkedIn's Tools

Once you click on a position that interests you, you will see a job description, a count of the number of people who have applied through LinkedIn, any of your connections that work there, and even other jobs openings at that company.

Importantly, LinkedIn will also tell you what skills you have that match the ones sought for the position. To the right of the job, look for the "How you match" section:

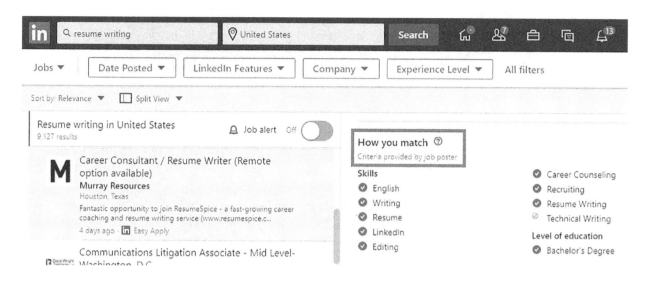

This section pulls the skills indicated as required by the job poster and matches them with the skills listed in your profile. If you match 80% of the skills, you're probably a good candidate for the position—you are qualified and also have some room to grow.

Premium members also have the added benefit of seeing how they rank compared to other potential applicants.

PREMIUM
Applicant rank
Top 10% of 47 applicants

If you are serious about applying to a particular job, use the "Apply/Easy Apply" or "Save" feature:

Once you save a job, you can find it from your jobs page:

You can view a list of all the jobs you've applied for from the Jobs tab at any time (under "Applied Jobs"). For more on how to work with Applied Jobs, see the LinkedIn Help article, Viewing Jobs You've Applied for on LinkedIn.[84]

"Easy Apply" is offered by businesses who use an applicant tracking system (ATS) to filter applications. LinkedIn hosts the application, "enabling you to pre-fill information from your profile to make it easier and faster to apply." Here's what the application looks like:

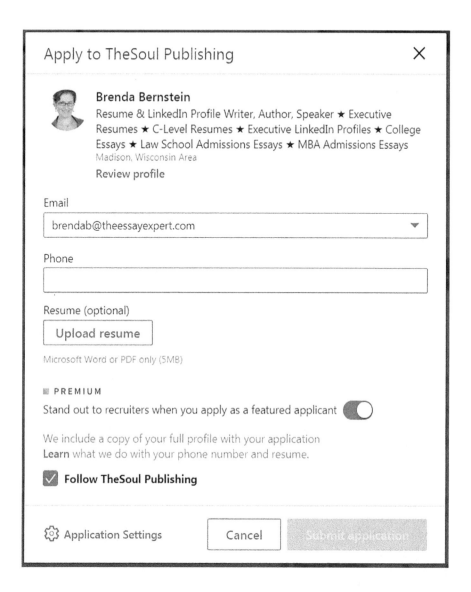

With a Premium account, you can get a lot of valuable information about the position you're applying for. Check this out as an example:

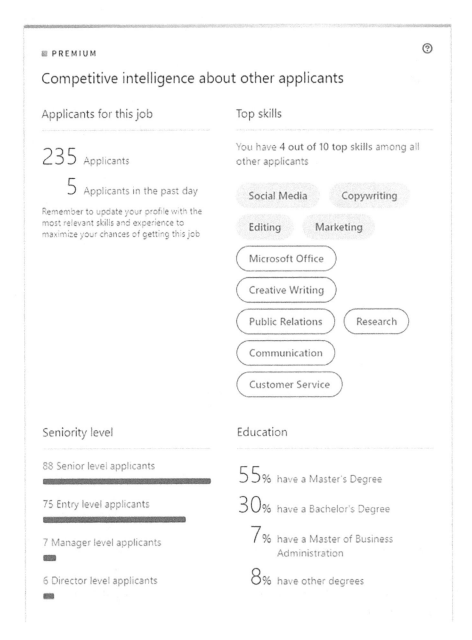

You can see how many people have applied for the position and how many have applied in the last day, so you know how competitive it is and whether applications are still coming in. And you can get a clear sense of who is applying and what skills you need to qualify for the position. If you have the skills required but they're not listed in your Skills section, add them before submitting your application!

LinkedIn Premium also allows you to see valuable insights about the company, its employees and its hiring trends. Plus you'll be able to view similar jobs that might interest you.

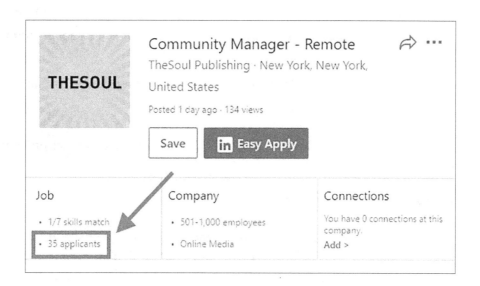

For more about the Easy Apply feature, see LinkedIn Help's article, "Apply to External Jobs Directly from LinkedIn - Frequently Asked Questions."[85]

What Recruiters See

When you apply with Easy Apply, recruiters and hiring reps will see the following information:

- Your name, headline, summary, current & past job titles, education, and recommendations
- Your connections, including mutual connections at the company
- Your contact information
- Your resume (if attached).
- Who you are following, what you're commenting on, and what you've shared.

I probably don't have to tell you that you want all this information to be available and complete. Make it easy for potential employers to find you and learn about you by having a complete profile, including your contact information in those fields, and staying active on LinkedIn.

What will turn recruiters and hiring managers off?

- Selfies or missing photos
- Dormant profiles (not responding to InMails, outdated info, minimal connections)
- Asking for free help, such as extensive resume/profile reviews, jobs (without establishing a connection and rapport first), etc.
- Bashing recruiters or your current company (always stay positive!)
- Liking, sharing, or commenting on inappropriate content
- Inconsistencies in your profile and resume

- Invalid contact info.

- Not reading job postings or hiring reps' profiles and therefore communicating inappropriately.

- Applying for every job posting (qualified or not).

- Responding negatively to rejection (posting, tagging, or sending InMails complaining about a rejection or sounding like a victim).

Enough said. Don't do the 10 things listed above! You'll just get the recruiter to click on "Not a fit" when they have a chance.

Should I Upload My Resume to LinkedIn?

LinkedIn gives you the option of uploading a resume to attach to your profile. If you do this, your resume will go out automatically with any job applications through LinkedIn. I highly recommend against doing this! Here's why:

If you apply through LinkedIn, a recruiter or hiring manager will always ask you for your resume—so you can tailor the document you send them to the position, as opposed to sending a "one-size-fits-all" resume. Also, for safety reasons, never attach a resume with your home address to your profile.

Again, I can't emphasize enough how important it is to be consistent with your job search. If you apply for every job in a company, from a mail clerk to a CEO, recruiters will see this and disregard your application. In contrast, if you are focused with the position you want, you will be seen as more attractive.

Even more attractive is applying to similar positions at the same company when you weren't selected the first time. Past applications may be seen as a positive indication of your true interest in working at the company and of your persistence and organization.

Share the Wealth!

Is a job not quite right for you but perfect for someone else in your network? Use LinkedIn's social media sharing buttons to spread the word.

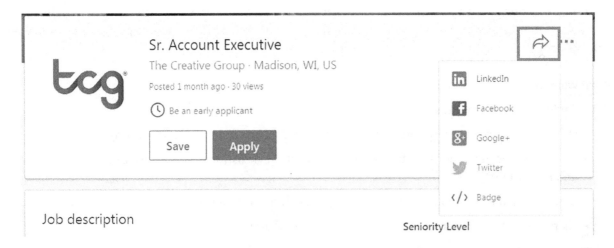

Do Your Research

To find out more about a job or company, reach out to the person who posted it. Or, if one job isn't the right fit, take a look at similar postings with the "People also viewed" or "Similar jobs" features:

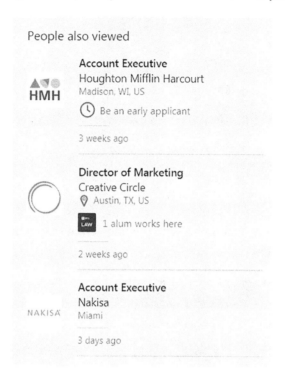

Scroll down to view a list of similar jobs:

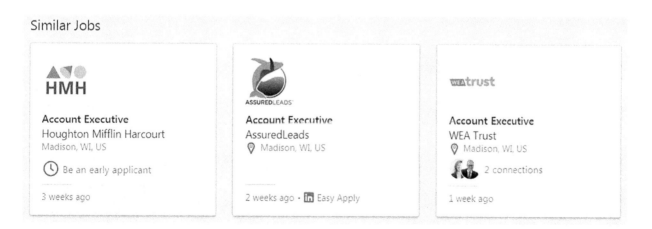

You can also search connections with similar titles. To see LinkedIn's Job Title Highlights, go to your Homepage and enter your desired title in the search bar. Then click on "People." You'll see that the People option is now a drop down—select "All."

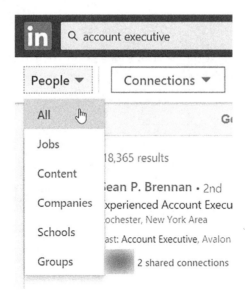

Now you'll see a list of LinkedIn members with the title you're searching for, top companies hiring for the position, and similar job titles.

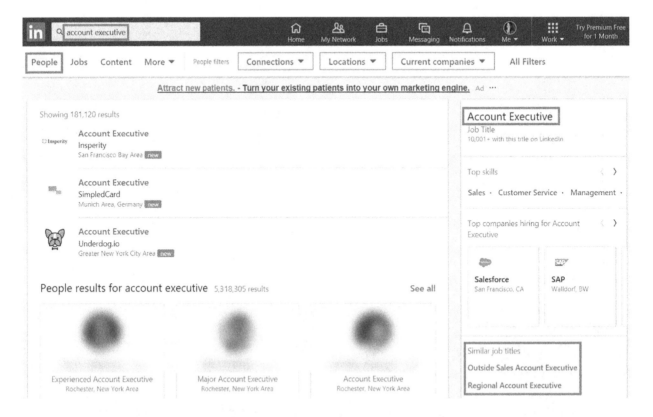

Interested in jobs similar to yours that pay more? For a limited time, LinkedIn will share those opportunities with you. To turn on this feature, called Salary Insights,[86] go to the Jobs tab and click on "LinkedIn Salary."[87]

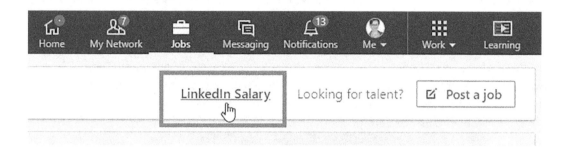

Scroll down to "Get the full picture" and click on "See more insights."

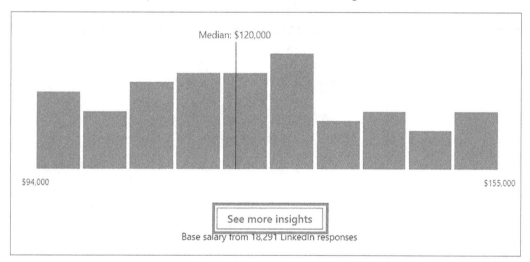

Complete the information and you'll see how you rank in salary with others in your position. You'll see top paying locations and clicking on these will provide a list of hiring companies in that area. Take advantage of this free tool while it lasts.

Tip Your Hand

You can let a company know you are interested in working for them by following the company on LinkedIn. Here are several reasons to follow a company, courtesy of WiserUTips:[88]

- **More visibility.** Representatives at your target companies can see who their followers are. By being on their followers list, you're telling companies that you are interested in them and you're also getting your skills and/or services in front of them.

- **Staying up-to-date.** View all recent updates about your target companies, including company news, job openings, new hires, and recent employee departures.

- **Making an impression.** Like and comment on posts about your target companies.

- **Making connections.** Review "How You're Connected." Click the "See all" link to view 1st, 2nd and 3rd degree connections at the organization, as well as former employees. Use this knowledge to ask key people to help you land a job or make the sale.

- **Showing your support.** Providing recommendations for a company's products and services makes the company look good on LinkedIn and shows them that you care about their success.

Hiring entities that use LinkedIn Recruiter can view those who follow their company. They will then consider you a "warm lead" and most likely check out your profile. Plus, you can follow up to 1,000 companies! The downside is that all your connections will also be able to see what companies you follow; so if you have an ummm, "overprotective" boss, be careful about how you use this feature.

Ask for a Referral

You can now easily ask for a referral from connections at a company you'd like to work for. Here's how:
Go to the Jobs tab and locate a job opening that interests you and also lists connections:

Once on the position's page, click "Ask for a referral."

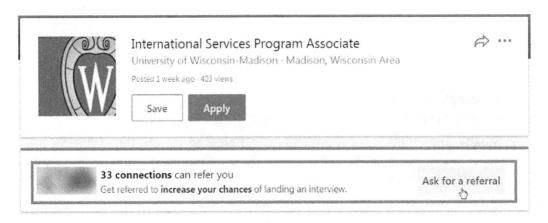

Select a connection you know well and click Message.

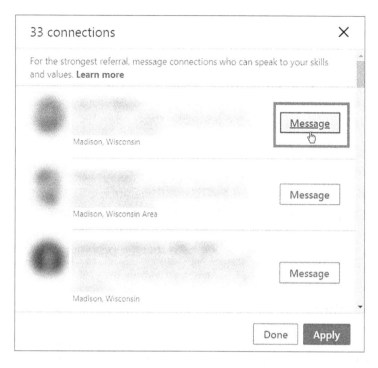

LinkedIn offers a ready-made message, or you can draft your own. The more personal, the better.

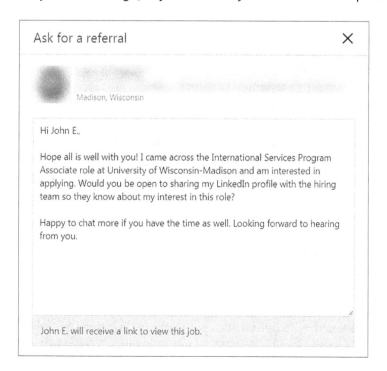

I highly recommend that you use this feature, since 85% of jobs are found through networking![89] What a goldmine!

LinkedIn Learning

Are you just a training or two short of being qualified for the positions you want? LinkedIn Learning might be a valuable resource for you. An online learning platform, LinkedIn Learning "enable[s] individuals and organizations to achieve their objectives and aspirations. [LinkedIn's] goal is to help people discover and develop the skills they need through a personalized, data-driven learning experience."

Both individual and organizational memberships are available for LinkedIn Learning. If you want to find out more, go to https://learning.linkedin.com/product-overview.

Talent Solutions

On the Company side, LinkedIn has created the "Next Generation of Career Pages."[90] If you are a job seeker, the new career pages could mean that you are getting a much better customer experience when a company is interested in your candidacy. You will be able to learn more about a company's culture, and have better access to people in similar roles to the ones that interest you. I'd love to hear your stories of how this feature works for you.

A Note on Contacting Recruiters

One way to find jobs on LinkedIn is through recruiters. Most of the time, contacting recruiters requires the use of InMail, which means you probably need to invest in a premium subscription. Job Search Premium also allows you to access metrics on why your application is not being selected; and there is evidence that you'll come up higher in recruiter searches.

Even without a premium subscription, you might be able to send an attention-getting connection request and communicate via regular messaging after that, but you'll have a more difficult time without InMail. As you can imagine, recruiters get bombarded by InMails and connection requests every day, and it truly takes something to grab their attention.

When you're not reaching out to friends who have an automatic personal connection with you, you need to establish one. Breaking through that barrier might be as simple as mentioning a mutual connection (someone you really know). Or you could refer to an article written by the person you want to connect with, or that mentions the person. All these points of connection can be found with simple LinkedIn searches.

If your LinkedIn investigations come up blank, try Googling the person and their company. Look at their blog if they have one, or their company website. You're likely to find some interesting information that you can use as a conversation starter. One LinkedIn user discovered a mutual interest in SCUBA diving with her intended connection and was able to get creative with that, going so far as to mention seahorses in her subject line! She got a response within 10 minutes.

If you're not so fortunate as to discover an eclectic mutual interest, you can always try the direct approach. Former recruiter Catherine Byers Breet suggests something like this: "I'm a healthcare data analyst. Do you ever need folks like me?"

Another pointer: The shorter the better. Start with your main point and don't go much beyond that. You'll need to catch their attention in the first 255 characters, which is what will appear in the notification about your message.

I highly recommend Byers Breet's article[91] for sample emails to recruiters that include humor and sizzle. Model after those, whether you're writing to a recruiter or someone else!

Tricks for Finding Hiring Reps – courtesy of Ashley Watkins of WriteStepResumes.com

If you want to contact a hiring rep outside of LinkedIn, try this tool for finding their company email address: Anymailfinder.com. This site shows the formula for company emails, e.g. First.Last@company.com. Often you'll get the correct formula and be able to reach a hiring rep directly.

Other sites and links that can help you find or verify someone's contact information:

- TruePeopleSearch.com
- Zabasearch.com
- Radaris.com
- search string: (contact OR email OR phone OR cell OR mobile) "john doe" "company name"
- VerifyEmailAddress.org

Here's a super-cool way to find hiring reps on LinkedIn who might be outside your 3rd degree connections. It's called the "X-ray technique." To work some serious LinkedIn magic, type into Google:

site:linkedin.com (inurl:pub) "executive recruiter" "new york" -jobs (the "-" means it's a parameter you don't want to search—so you can put anything in here that you don't want to come up in your results.)

Here are my results:

10+ Rachel Rosin profiles | LinkedIn
https://www.linkedin.com/pub/dir/Rachel/Rosin
Current Senior Executive Recruiter at Diamond Staffing Solutions, Inc. ... Education, City University of **New York** City College, The Bronx High School of Science ...

Ken Kupersmith - Executive Recruiter, BioPharma Medical/Regulatory ...
https://tf.linkedin.com/pub/
***BioPharma Medical/Regulatory Affairs Executive Recruiter at
specializing in placing ... Région de **New York** City, États-Unis.

2500+ Dee Dee Dee profiles in Greater New York City Area | LinkedIn
https://www.linkedin.com/pub/dir/Dee+Dee.../+/us-70-Greater-New-York-City-Area
Current Executive Recruiter- Insurance Industry- at **New York**. Past, Sales Accounting Manager at Computer Associates, **New York**, Accounting Manager at ...

Top 25 Steve Lee profiles | LinkedIn
https://www.linkedin.com/pub/dir/Steve/Lee ▾
Past, Agent NJ# 1671082 at **New York** Life Insurance Company Executive Recruiter (NYC) / Managing Director (Seoul, S. Korea) at AppleOne - Act-1.

20+ Daniel Persons profiles | LinkedIn
https://www.linkedin.com/pub/dir/Daniel/Persons
Current Executive Recruiter at Towerhill Associates, **Executive Recruiter** at ... Current, Consultant at Foot Center of **New York**, Broker at NY State Health ...

I'd love to hear what results you get by using this trick!

The Tune-Up for Employers/Recruiters

If you have a company page on LinkedIn, after clicking on the Jobs tab, you will see an "Are you hiring?" section in the top right corner:

Click on the "Post a job" button and you will be brought to another screen where you be asked to supply information about the company and position.

Note that posting a job is not free. For more details, see LinkedIn Help article, Posting a Job on LinkedIn.[92]

Posting a job on LinkedIn provides credibility to your company that will attract top candidates. Simply put, in my opinion LinkedIn is one of the best job boards currently in existence. Where else do you get such complete information on both candidates and companies? If I were looking for an employee, I would not hesitate to post the opening on LinkedIn. Even if referrals are your best source of job candidates, LinkedIn is a central place to get the word out.

The advantages of posting jobs on LinkedIn:

1. You can forward the job posting easily to your 1st degree connections to spread the word and generate referrals.

2. You can share the posting easily with your LinkedIn groups, LinkedIn Network, Facebook and Twitter.

3. You can link a job posting to your profile so that everyone who views your profile sees the job posting.

4. The Recommended matches feature provides the best candidates matched to your position.

5. There's a 10-applicant guarantee for members who have not previously posted a job on LinkedIn.

6. When you post a job, an update will go to all your 1st degree connections.

7. Candidates are automatically asked to upload their resume and cover letter. Once someone applies, you get an email with a summary of the applicant's LinkedIn profile and all the documents they submitted; you can then review their full profile if you'd like.

8. When a new applicant applies, you get a link to view all the candidates who have applied for the job to date. You will find this feature very useful!

9. LinkedIn is probably the best database of professionals worldwide in just about any industry. If your candidate is not leveraging LinkedIn, they might not be the right candidate.

Note that if you have purchased a Gold or Silver Career page for your Company page, featured jobs will be displayed on that page and will be targeted to viewers based on how relevant their profile is to the job posted. This function provides tremendous screening value to you as an employer or recruiter.

LinkedIn has also made "limited listings" available to its job-seeking members. Not to be confused with Job Slots or Job Posts which are visible to all job seekers, limited listings are job listings aggregated from sources outside of LinkedIn that are displayed only to members who are the most relevant candidates for the position, based on their profile content and the employer's criteria.

Group Job Postings

You can post jobs in your groups. After logging into one of your group pages, click on the field to "Start a new conversation in this group," and post your job opening. Click Post and the job will appear in the group's feed.

Results to Expect

The evidence, based on my own client base, is that more and more qualified job seekers are finding employment by diligently applying for jobs on LinkedIn. This is good news for both applicants and employers. Whether you are looking for a position or looking to fill one, LinkedIn is a powerful tool to achieve your intended result.

If you are a job seeker, and if you look in LinkedIn® Jobs daily and apply for positions appropriate to your background, you will likely see results! I have one client who got 12 interviews that way, and a job!

Mistake #17

No Recommendations, Very Few Recommendations, and/or Boring or Error-Filled Recommendations

The Problem

Profiles with recommendations rank more highly in searches than those with the exact same keywords but without recommendations. Members with recommendations are also three times more likely to be contacted. If you are short on recommendations from your connections, people might wonder whether they can truly trust you.

There is some evidence that search results are ranked partly by how many recommendations you have. If this rumor is true, then fewer recommendations can mean lower ranking.

As Laurie Phillips,[93] business consultant and CEO at Sundance Research, offers: "Even if candidates don't give me their LinkedIn profile link, I check them out here [because] LinkedIn gives me descriptive personal references that corporations typically prohibit. Even though I know those references are biased toward the positive, they give me some idea of your personality."

With the advent of Endorsements (for more about Endorsements, see **Mistake #12**), it might be tempting to rely on those easily checked boxes and become complacent about requesting more personal recommendations. Don't be lulled! Endorsements take no energy on the part of the person making the endorsement, and sometimes people who cannot actually vouch for your skills endorse you for those skills.

Also note: Errors and poor writing, or simply a lack of spark in your recommendations, reflect poorly on both you and the recommender—and the recommendation can backfire. So demand excellence in your recommendations!

The Tune-Up

Whether you own a business or are looking for work, recommendations are an opportunity to have people sell you—so you don't have to do all the selling yourself.

You have the opportunity on LinkedIn to request recommendations from people you know: your colleagues, clients, supervisors, or even staff. Don't be shy! Write to your connections and ask them to recommend you.

I recommend displaying at least 5 recommendations, with 5-10 being ideal for most professionals. Many hiring professionals agree, "The more the merrier!"

Requesting Recommendations

You will find the option to request or offer recommendations when you are viewing anyone's profile. Just click on the "More" button in the person's introduction card:

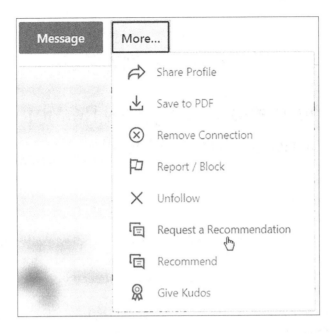

If you want the person (in this case "Chris") to recommend you, choose "Request a recommendation" and you'll be brought to this screen:

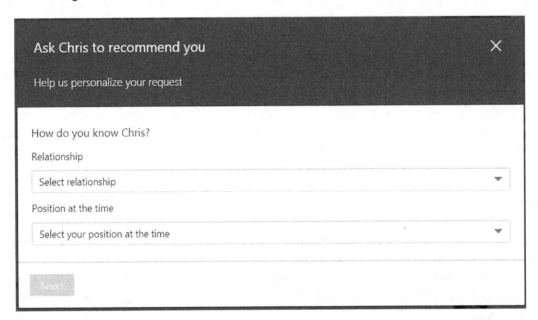

Another way to request a recommendation is to scroll down to the Recommendations section of your own profile and click on "Ask for a recommendation":

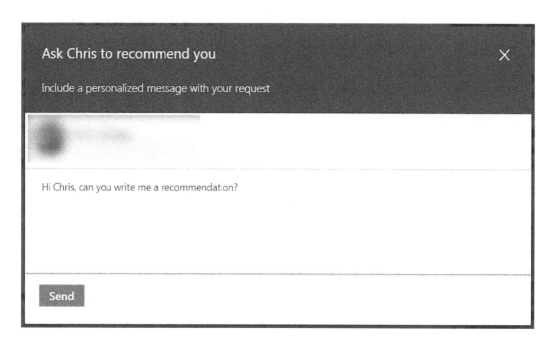

Don't simply use the default message here ("Hi [Name], can you write me a recommendation?"). Instead, say hello to the person and ask how he or she is doing (or, ideally, do this by phone before asking for the recommendation at all). If you haven't been in contact for some time, remind this colleague, boss, or other connection of a project you worked on together, a deal you made, or something else that will refresh their recollection of your professional skills. Then ask your recommender to tell a clear, specific story or two about you (positive ones of course). Examples of how you handled a situation, what you accomplished, or how you helped someone are always more informative and interesting than generalizations!

Consider, if you have more than 10 recommendations, whether you are displaying too many (the answer to this question will depend on your situation). If I applied at your company and gave you 150 letters of recommendation, how much attention would you pay to each one?

You can save all recommendations and display the ones you choose at any given time. You may choose to display certain recommendations when job seeking, others when starting a new business.

To show or hide your recommendations, click on the pencil icon:

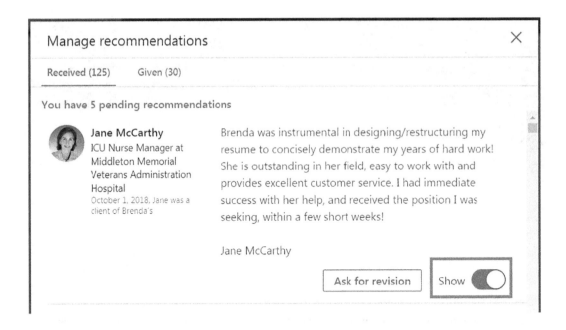

The default is to show the recommendation. If you do not want to display it, click the "Show" slider to change it to "Hide" and the recommendation will be hidden (see above example).

If you prefer to display recommendations other than the ones that appear by default on your profile, you can hide them; but then no one will be able to view the hidden recommendations and they will NOT be counted in the number of recommendations displayed on your profile.

Accepting or Revising Recommendations

Once you receive a recommendation, you should be notified in your inbox.

You can also check your pending recommendations by clicking the link in your Recommendation section:

Or visit this direct link: https://www.linkedin.com/recs/received.

You'll have the opportunity to accept or dismiss the recommendation. If there is an error or something you'd rather that someone say differently, you can ask your recommender to correct it, which I encourage you to do if what they wrote is not exactly the way you want it! Just click the "Ask for revision" button.

Also, make sure each recommendation says something compelling about you—that it tells a story of some sort and could not have been written about anyone else. Most people are very cooperative when you make a request for a replacement. Remember, the recommendations say as much about the recommender as they do about you! If you're afraid to request a replacement, just tell them I sent you.

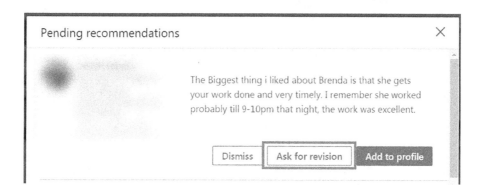

Accompany your request with a copy of the original recommendation and your suggested changes so your recommender does not have to start from scratch.

Here's a before and after example from one of my clients:

Before: "Besides really enjoying the time with Mary, her knowledge of Networking opportunities were invaluable. We related very well and her training techniques were easy to follow. This opened up a whole new world of networking opportunity which will be pursue with vigor. I look forward to continuing a working relationship with her."

After: "Not only was Mary enjoyable to work with, but her knowledge of Networking was invaluable. We related very well and her training techniques were easy to follow. She opened up a whole new world of networking opportunities which our company will pursue with vigor."

If you're writing a recommendation, this tip applies to you. Craft it well, as it reflects on you as much as on the person you're recommending. Only recommend people whose work you truly know!

Reordering Recommendations

LinkedIn used to allow reordering of Recommendations and have hinted that this feature may return, but for now, Recommendations are ordered by the date they are accepted. The ones attached to your current experience will also get priority. Some workarounds:

1. Hide the recommendations you don't like as much, so your favorites rise to the top of the list.

2. Use the "Request a Revision" feature to ask your connection if they would submit their recommendation again. Once you have accepted it anew, it will appear at the top.

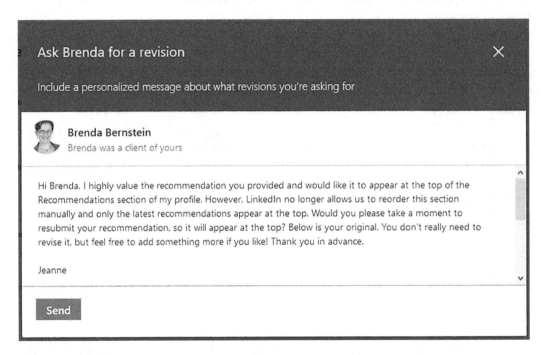

3. Delete an old position with an important recommendation attached to it. The recommendation will become free to reassign to other positions. It would be a rare instance, however, where an old recommendation is also applicable to a new one.

Tracking Your LinkedIn Recommendations

Want a quick run-down of all your received and given recommendations? Scroll down in your profile and here's what you'll see:

Recommendations   Ask for a recommendation ✎

Received (125)   Given (30)

Or, want to see all the recommendation requests people have sent you? Go to https://www.linkedin.com/recs/received.

Recommendation Challenges

Here are some issues that commonly come up with people on my LinkedIn webinars:

1. "I haven't talked to my recommender in 10 years . . . I would be so embarrassed to ask!"

In this situation, think about how you would respond if the tables were turned. Wouldn't you be happy to hear from someone who did good work for you or who was a great boss or colleague 10 years ago? If you thought highly of the person, wouldn't you be happy to provide a recommendation? And seriously, what's the worst that can happen? They don't respond or they say no? In that case, you won't be any worse off than you are without their recommendation now!

2. "My recommenders aren't on LinkedIn."

In this situation, there are at least three options that can address the issue:

- Invite the person onto LinkedIn. It might be just the nudge your recommender needs to join the millions of LinkedIn users!

- Attach your recommendation under the relevant job as a link or file, using the instructions in **Mistake #15**. If you do this, you may want to write a line in that section directing readers to view your attached recommendations.

- Include the recommendation in the summary or experience section of your profile. Most people will trust that it's real, though some might be more trusting of a recommendation that comes through LinkedIn's official Recommendations system. If the comment is persuasive and flows in the context of the section, I say go ahead and type it in! Here's an example of what it might look like (at the end of the Summary) from Robin Rice of Be Who You Are Productions, Inc.:[94]

WHOLE-LIFE SYSTEMS ✴ THINKING PARTNER TO LEADERS AND INFLUENCERS

I offer personal and professional support to high profile executives, artists, civic leaders, and entrepreneurs—change agents who find themselves in search of insight, perspective, next-level thinking and expanded personal truth.

✹ FROM PREVIOUS CLIENTS ✹

"I'm left to marvel at all that has changed and all that has happened over the past six months: much better sleep, far less anxiety, a book deal with a major publisher, a glowing review for my current book in the Washington Post, a new business plan that is as surprising as it is exciting. I've kept the weight off. My relationship with my wife has never been better. And I'm in a consistent creative zone the likes of which I've never known before. The bottom line: I just feel better. I'm happier, day in and day out."

— Matthew S., Author & Entrepreneur

"Big thanks to Robin Rice for compassionately coaching me through my resistance . . ."

— Arielle Ford, Author, Wabi-Sabi Love

**Note: There are three downsides to these last two options: 1) Theoretically, you could make the recommendation up; 2) It is harder for viewers to find the recommendation; and 3) The recommendation will not be counted by LinkedIn so will not show up in your number of recommendations received.

3. "My previous company has a policy against recommendations."

If your past supervisors are precluded from recommending you due to company policy, you might have hit a dead end—but your coworkers might still be able to write a recommendation; and keep track of those supervisors, as they might move to a new company and be freed up to write a recommendation for you. Pay attention to the daily emails you receive with updates and look for news about potential recommenders!

Note that some supervisors, even if they are not officially permitted to recommend you, might sign a letter of recommendation that you draft for them. Or if you present such a letter to them, they might decide to write one themselves. This type of thing happens more often than you think! So even if you can't extract a public LinkedIn recommendation from someone, see if you can get an old-fashioned letter!

4. "My best recommendations are getting pushed to the bottom."

For tips on how to handle this issue, see Reordering Recommendations, above. Note that one of these options requires reaching out to your recommender for an update. I would approach this issue by telling your recommender how much you value what they wrote, and that you want their recommendation to appear at the top of your profile. Compliments will get you everywhere!

Giving Recommendations

I encourage you to recommend people as well as to request recommendations. It feels great to help someone out, and if you have your Privacy settings set to share your profile edits, your connections will get notified that you recommended someone. Plus, recruiters like to see that you've recommended people in addition to having received recommendations.

Word to the wise: Make sure to have some "one-way" recommendations, as "mutual" or "reciprocal" recommendations are often not as highly trusted.

Here's how to give a recommendation:

If you want to recommend Chris, go to his profile and click "Recommend."

You'll be brought to a page with this start box:

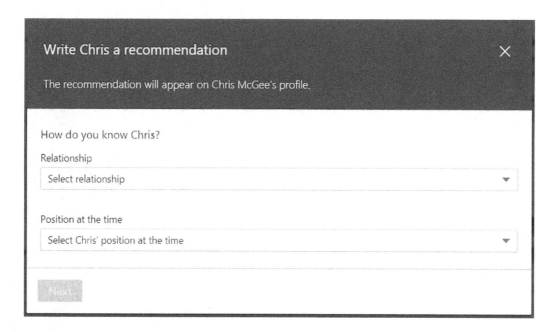

You can also view Recommendation requests by adding /detail/recommendations/requests/ to the end of your LinkedIn profile URL.

Write something that will support the person you're recommending with some concrete examples of their strengths, written in a way that also reflects favorably upon you. You might want to get your recommendation edited by someone you trust. You don't to inadvertently post anything with a typo!

I've always liked the saying, "Give until it feels good." Giving recommendations on LinkedIn is a great way to create positive feelings for both yourself and others!

Results to Expect

By giving and accumulating recommendations, you will build positive relationships with people in your network while also gaining the trust of potential employers, clients, and whomever else you want to impress on LinkedIn—trust that can translate into business or into a job. I have had many people choose to work with The Essay Expert based on the strength of the recommendations posted on my LinkedIn profile. Imagine, if you are a business or sales person, having clients come to you already having decided you're the person they want to work with!

Recommending people can also get you attention from recruiters. Read Are LinkedIn Recommendations Important? Here's What 10 Hiring Managers Say[95] for some insightful views from recruiters on how much weight recommendations hold when choosing the right candidate. Also, it's a little-known fact that recruiters search on the recommendations you've given, not just on the ones you receive! You will be seen and recognized as a team player if you give great recommendations to people you know.

If your recommendations are compelling and error-free, both you and your recommenders will make a great impression. The strength of your recommendations can get you your next client or your next job.

Mistake #18

A Static (Unchanging, Outdated) Profile—and Thinking all You Need is a KILLER LinkedIn Profile

The Problem

Your LinkedIn profile is not a static, unchanging document. Members expect to find up to date information there! You wouldn't send out a resume without your most current position listed, or with past positions listed as if they are current. Why would you have a LinkedIn profile with outdated information?

If you earned a degree in 2018 and haven't worked since 2015, it would be a shame to forget to list those three years you were in school! You could appear to be unemployed when you really were a hard-working student that whole time.

If "Sharing profile edits" in your Settings & Privacy is set to "Yes," every time you update your profile, a message goes out to all your connections. If you don't update your profile, this feature won't help you and your connections won't be updated on your career milestones.

Let's face it: Even if you have the most amazing LinkedIn profile in the world, you won't get results by sitting there doing nothing.

The Tune-Up

Regularly update your Headline, Summary, Experience (Job Titles) and Education sections. Add accomplishments when you achieve new ones. Join new groups. Make and request new recommendations. Post links and Activity Updates relevant to who you are and what you're up to. Stay active.

If you are afraid you are making *too* many changes, and that your connections will get annoyed, turn off your notifications before you make profile changes. You can access this feature at the bottom of the pop-up window any time you add a new section to your profile:

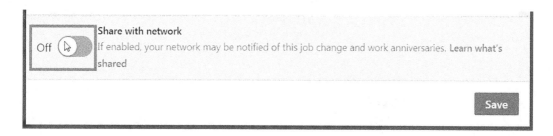

Or, go to the Settings & Privacy tab, which you will find under your photo in the right-hand corner of your homepage:

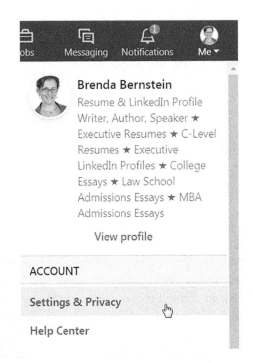

Navigate to "Sharing profile edits" and switch it to No.

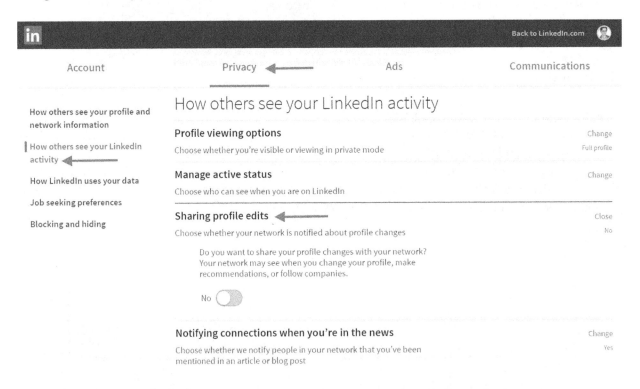

Remember to Update!

If you tend to forget that your LinkedIn profile exists, you might want to put a tickler in your calendar reminding you to update your profile at least every month. Also, read articles about new features on LinkedIn and about how to write a great profile. Update your profile according to what you learn. Reading this book—and future editions—is a great first step.

Finally, unless you stay active in groups, conversations, and . . . most important . . . OFF LINE, you will not get the greatest possible results out of your LinkedIn profile.

LinkedIn provides a wealth of information about every one of your contacts. Be an explorer!

Read through someone's entire profile before starting a conversation. You may discover videos and other documents in addition to basic education and employment information. If they have recommended people, you can get insight into their values system. If they have received multiple recommendations, you'll get a sense of their greatest strengths. Do they volunteer somewhere? If so, talking about their volunteer experience can be a great icebreaker.

Get Personal

Pay attention to your Notifications page where you get notifications of people's birthdays and job changes/anniversaries. Respond to them! Don't forget to write comments, post questions, give and receive recommendations and endorsements . . . and ask people you want to truly connect with to talk with you on the phone or even meet you for coffee or lunch.

Ready to meet with someone? Sync your calendar to LinkedIn. LinkedIn will provide your contact's details and also remind you to follow up after the meeting. To use this feature, go to your profile by clicking on your picture. Tap on the gear to the right of your name and then tap Sync calendar. For a quick video on how to sync your calendar on an Android device, see LinkedIn's article, Tuesday Tip: Prepare for the Day with LinkedIn Calendar Sync.[96]

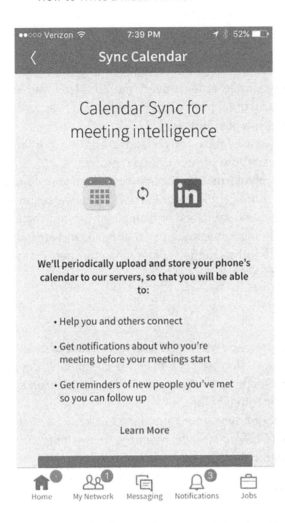

To learn more about this feature, visit LinkedIn's Help article, "Syncing Your Calendar in the LinkedIn Mobile App."[97]

Results to Expect

By staying updated and active, you will likely get emails from your connections congratulating you on your new position, your new accomplishment, or the new look of your profile. You will be seen as someone who is active in your profession and serious about your online presentation. Not only that, but if you comment on people's news, they will like you (and I don't mean click on the "like" button. I mean actually like you)! Who doesn't appreciate getting congratulated or being wished a happy birthday?

See how you're doing at making business connections by checking your Social Selling Index (you may need to paste this URL directly into your browser: https://www.linkedin.com/sales/ssi).

According to LinkedIn, "Salespeople who excel at social selling are creating more opportunities and are 51% more likely to hit quota."[98]

Here's what your score will look like:

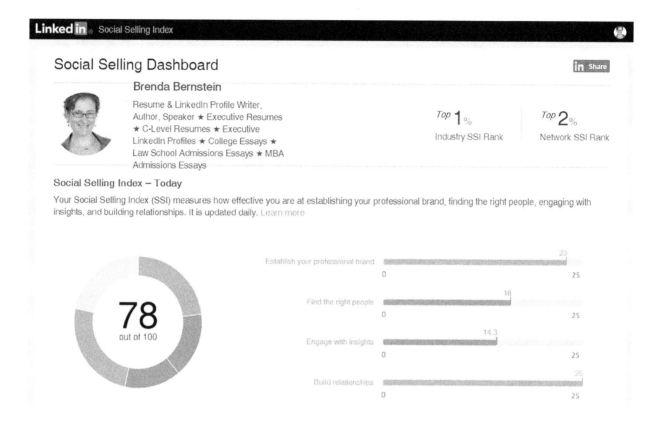

To find read more about this feature, read Get Your Score: LinkedIn Makes the Social Selling Index Available for Everyone.[99]

The Power of Connections

The more activity you generate, the more people will view your profile and the more likely you are to make connections.

I'll tell you a secret: A huge proportion of my business was built because I was active in a group and the manager of the group connected me with one of its other members who lives in Austin, Texas. I happened to be visiting Austin and met with that member, and he was so impressed with our meeting that he began referring me multiple clients and giving me opportunities to present webinars with his company. That connection led to webinars and a huge expansion of brand awareness for me and my company.

More recently, on a trip to New York and New Haven, I met in person with three connections I had initially met via LinkedIn. All three meetings led to results I never would have imagined—results that probably would not have manifested if we had kept our communications to LinkedIn and telephone.

Please take my story to heart. Don't stop at online LinkedIn connections! Bring them to the next level with a phone call or in-person meeting, and the possibilities are endless.

Bonus Tip #1

Save Your Work . . . and Your Connections!

The Problem

LinkedIn is not a perfect system, and there have been stories of disappearing profiles. If you haven't saved the results of all your hard work, you can lose it. I'm guessing that would be aggravating for you. Furthermore, if your profile gets axed for any reason, you could easily lose your hundreds or thousands of LinkedIn connections.

The Tune-Up

To retain the results of your labors, back up your profile!

LinkedIn has created a way for you to save all your information in one fell swoop by requesting an archive of your data.

To request your archive, go to your Settings & Privacy and click the Privacy tab, then "How LinkedIn uses your data." Select "The works":

You will need to enter your password, then click "Request archive" to complete your request and wait! If you have a lot of connections, your archive might be split into two parts.

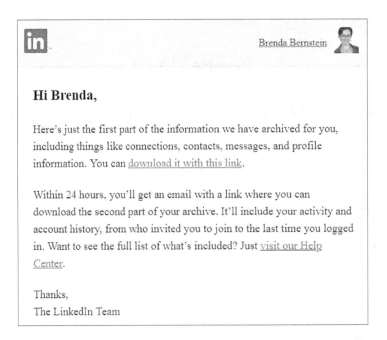

You should receive your download file within 24 hours—and you might be excited to see all the information it contains—including a complete history of your account activity, a list of your connections, your endorsements and recommendations, and more! For a list of everything that's exported, visit LinkedIn's help center article regarding downloading your account data.[100] I personally discovered the following:

1. My LinkedIn account was created 5/21/08 and I was invited by an old acquaintance, to whom I wrote a quick thank you as soon as I got my archive!

2. This is a great way to export a connections list (see Exporting Connections Only below)!

3. The first time I requested this archive, I had created 1940 group posts. By the end of 2018, I had created 3050!

Exporting Profile Only

On your View Profile page (in the Profile drop-down), click on the "More" button below a connection's headline to open a drop-down with an option "Save to PDF."

Save the document that gets generated and you will instantly have a record of all the fruits of your labors.

You'll have something that looks like this:

Contact

608-467-0067 (Work)
brendab@theessayexpert.com

www.linkedin.com/in/
brendabernstein (LinkedIn)
www.TheEssayExpert.com (Other)
www.TheExecutiveExpert.com
(Other)
killerlinkedinprofile.com (Other)

Top Skills

Resume Writing

Executive Resumes

C-Level Resumes

Certifications

Certified Master Resume Writer
(CMRW)

Certified Executive Resume Master
(CERM)

Honors-Awards

TORI Award Winner, Best New
Graduate Resume, 3rd Place

TORI Award Nominee, Best Re-
Entry Resume

TORI Award Nominee, Best Creative
Resume

Certified Master Resume Writer
(CMRW)

Publications

How to Write a WINNING Resume:
50 Tips to Reach Your Job Search
Target

How to Write a KILLER LinkedIn
Profile - E-Book

How to Write a STELLAR Executive
Resume: 60 Tips to Reach Your Job
Search Target

The Essay Expert Blog | Resumes |
LinkedIn | Personal Statements

Brenda Bernstein

Resume & LinkedIn Profile Writer, Author, Speaker ★ Executive
Resumes ★ C-Level Resumes ★ Executive LinkedIn Profiles
★ College Essays ★ Law School Admissions Essays ★ MBA
Admissions Essays
Madison, Wisconsin Area

Summary

▸ Stop struggling to write about yourself! And start looking great on
paper.

The Essay Expert works personally and intensively with Executive-
level job seekers, and college/MBA/law school applicants, to define
and express your essence. We create powerfully written resumes,
LinkedIn profiles and bios that spark the interest of hiring managers
and universities.

If you are not getting the results you want with your Executive
resume, LinkedIn profile or application essay, contact us for
professional writing and coaching services--and start moving your
career to the next level.

BRENDA BERNSTEIN & THE ESSAY EXPERT TEAM

Brenda is one of a handful of Certified Master Resume Writers
(CMRWs) and Certified Executive Resume Masters (CERMs)
worldwide. She holds an English degree from Yale and a J.D. from
NYU, both with honors. Her team of award-winning writers insert the
"wow" factor into every client's writing project!

OUR PROFESSIONAL WRITING SERVICES

▸ Resume Writing | Executive | Board Resumes
Your resume is your first opportunity to impress a potential employer,
a board, and your network. We make sure you stand out from the
competition. No templates! Executive Resume Specialist.

▸ LinkedIn Profile Writing & Coaching

Repeat this export process every time you make a change to your profile.

Exporting Connections Only

Note that as of December 2018, your connections export will contain a limited number of email addresses. This is due to LinkedIn's change to member privacy settings, which makes email addresses not download-able by default. I'm happy about this change since it will prevent a lot of the spamming that occurs on LinkedIn; but it also makes it more of a challenge for me to communicate with my LinkedIn connections outside of LinkedIn.

If you want others to be able to download your email, go to Settings & Privacy under "Who can see your email address" and switch it to Yes. And if you want to send a blast to your LinkedIn connections, well, you'll have to populate most of the list by hand now.

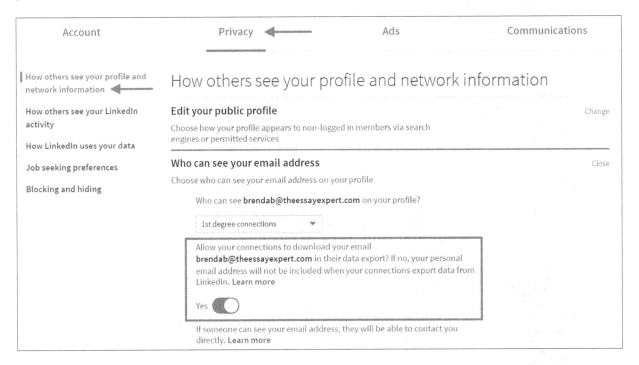

To save your LinkedIn connections, click on My Network:

Then click on your number of connections in the left sidebar:

In the upper right of the following page, find "Manage synced and imported contacts."

In the right sidebar, click on "Export contacts."

Choose "Connections" then click "Request Archive."

Your file will be emailed to you, usually within the day. You will then have the first name, last name and email address of every person in your LinkedIn contact list. Do NOT use this list to send out spam emails! Be courteous please.

Note: If you are exporting your connections to a Mac and you use Mac mail, connections will export directly to your address book (not an Excel spreadsheet). When prompted to import them into your contacts, you may think you are duplicating them, however, they will be saved as a "Smart Group." For more instructions on exporting connections to your Mac, read, How to Manually Import LinkedIn Contacts into Mac Contacts.[101]

Results to Expect

A recoverable profile and a secure contacts list. Peace of mind.

Bonus Tip #2

For Businesses: Ensure Brand Consistency—and Create a Company Page

The Problem

According to Small Business Trends[102] and a 2016 study conducted by TrackMaven, LinkedIn crushes other social media platforms when it comes to company page followers.

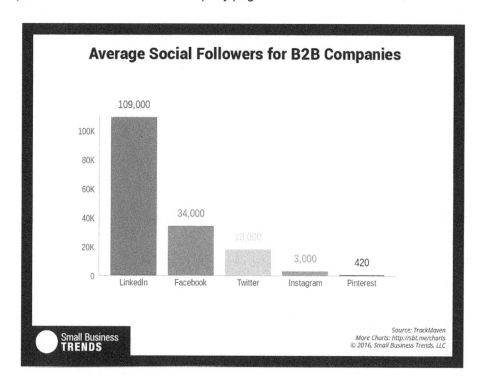

If you own a company, you want your employees to have profiles that build your brand. If they are misspelling your company name or creating job descriptions willy-nilly, you lose out on brand consistency.

And if all you have on LinkedIn is a personal profile and the personal profiles of your employees, how will people find your company? They certainly won't find you when searching the company pages.

More than 4 million companies have LinkedIn Pages.[103] If you're not one of them, you are missing out not just on LinkedIn searchability but on Google search results, where your rankings will suffer.

The Tune-Up

Take some time to create consistency across your employees' profiles. I don't advocate becoming "Big Brother" and keeping close watch at all times over the people working at your company; LinkedIn is indeed a job search tool and I believe you have to accept that employees might use it for that purpose. (My philosophy: Focus on keeping your employees happy rather than preventing them from exploring other opportunities!) More important in my book is that you create a culture of trust by working together with your teams to create a consistent brand and to form community on LinkedIn. Build optimized profiles for company leadership, for all existing employees, and for all new employees, and continue to train your staff on LinkedIn best practices. I believe the benefits to your company will outweigh any risks. A great article on this topic from Forbes can be found at Why Every Employee At Your Company Should Use LinkedIn.[104]

In addition to building consistent management and staff profiles, you must have a company page.[105] To create one, click on your "Work" icon in the upper right navigation bar and select "Create a Company Page" from the drop-down menu.

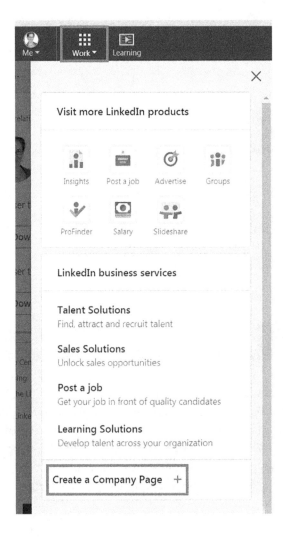

You will be brought to a screen that looks like this:

Add your company name, select your custom company profile URL, verify that you are the official rep for the company, and click " Create page." (You no longer need to have an email address at the company, but you do need to have a verified email address associated with a LinkedIn account.) LinkedIn provides some helpful tips to get you started:

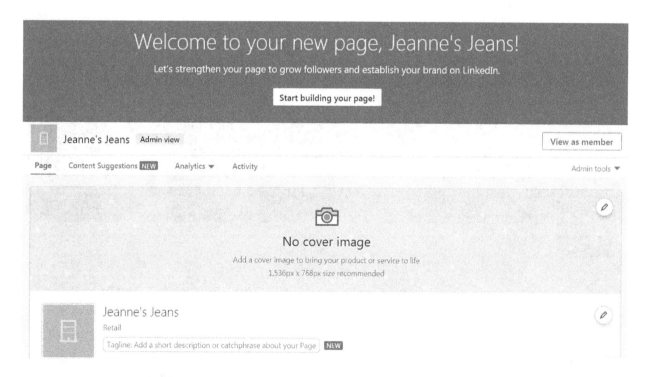

LinkedIn has made it possible to create a very attractive company profile whether or not you purchase their premium service.

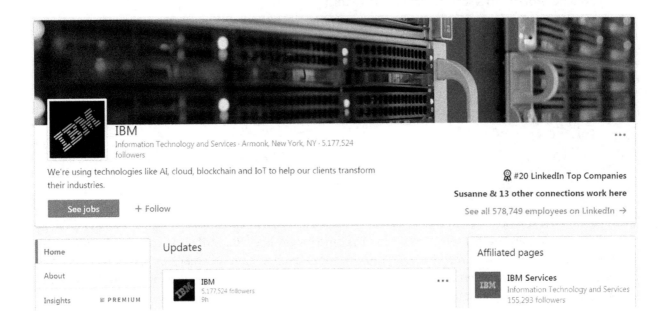

[You may notice that some company pages boast an animated logo. Sadly, this feature is no longer available, as LinkedIn has discontinued the ability to upload GIFs as company logos.]

You can promote specialized products or services with Showcase Pages. For example:

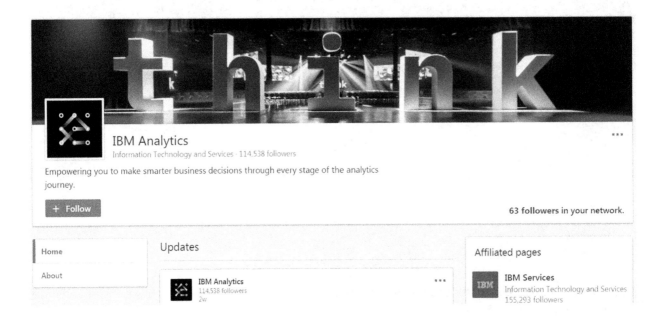

To create a Showcase page, first go to your Company Profile page by clicking on "Me" in the upper right of your menu bar and selecting your company:

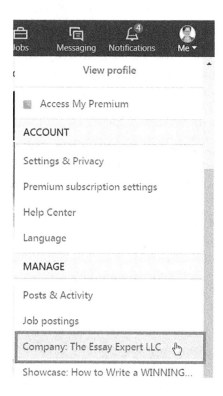

From your Company page, click on the "Admin tools" drop-down and select "Create a Showcase Page."

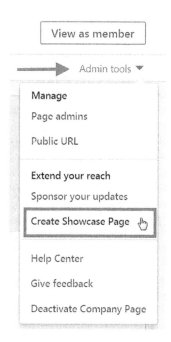

You can further optimize your page by including keywords in your product/service description. You have 200 characters to do so.

You can have up to 10 Company Showcase pages. Here's what you can do on those pages:

- Post videos and important updates regarding your featured product/service.
- Identify a specific audience to whom you want to promote your product or service based on company size, job function, industry, seniority, and geography.
- Create specific videos tailored to your chosen audience.
- Pin an introductory post at the top of each page.

Interested viewers can follow your page and receive updates in their homepage feed. If you succeed in creating buzz around your offerings, you will be well on your way to being a LinkedIn company superstar! For more on Showcase Pages, see LinkedIn Help's, "Showcase Pages - Overview."[106]

Staying Active with Your Company Page

You can post status updates for your company just as you would for yourself and keep your followers informed of all your latest news! Some things you might want to share include news/press about your company, job openings or new products/services offered. Keep your posts short and include videos whenever possible. Use LinkedIn's tools to target different audiences and track metrics on your posts.

LinkedIn's Content Suggestions is a curated list of trending content LinkedIn thinks you might like to comment on and/or share with your company page followers. Note that this feature is only available for Company pages with a following of 300 or more. For more about how to make the most of this feature, read LinkedIn Help's article, Using Content Suggestions on Your LinkedIn Page.[107]

Use the time or resources you have dedicated to LinkedIn activities to engage in conversation with followers—an essential part of a customer service strategy.

Company Page Resources

You can change your company page settings from your main company page, share from the Content Suggestions tab, see how your page is doing with Analytics, or review your latest activity from the Activity tab. For more information on setting up and leveraging company pages, see LinkedIn's Company Pages FAQ.[108]

Results to Expect

Your company will present a professional and savvy image on LinkedIn. The company will be searchable on LinkedIn not only in multiple ways: through your profile and the profiles of your employees, and also through Company Pages. This multiple exposure will boost your company in LinkedIn's search rankings *as well as on Google.*

Good news: LinkedIn currently has the highest lead conversion rate of any social media platform. According to one study, 5000+ businesses reported that LinkedIn enjoyed an average 2.74% visitor to conversion ratio, as opposed to 0.69% for Twitter and 0.77% for Facebook. Another study showed that

LinkedIn was responsible for landing 64% of social referrals on business home pages. Facebook and Twitter were far less effective at 17% and 14% respectively.

More traffic to your website means more sales. Don't miss out on this opportunity for FREE marketing and Search Engine Optimization! For the metrics-minded, you'll be happy to know that LinkedIn provides analytics for your page's activities!

To view them, go to your Analytics page as described above. You'll be able to review these metrics:

- Statistics on all the updates you've posted, including impressions (or reach) and percent engagement.

- Demographics and trends of your followers, including how you compare with similar companies.

- Visitor statistics and demographics.

Here's a sample from the end of October 2018:

Use these statistics to identify your target audience and measure what activity has generated the most views of your page. Then do more of what's working to build your audience and client base!
Learn more about LinkedIn Company page best practices here.[109]

Bonus Tip #3

Create a Profile Badge

The Problem

If an employer or client receives any online document from you and wants to look at your LinkedIn profile, you want to make it easy for them to do so.

The Tune-Up

To create an email signature that links to your LinkedIn profile page, click "Edit public profile & URL" in the upper right of your profile page:

Then scroll down to the bottom of the right sidebar and click "Create a badge."

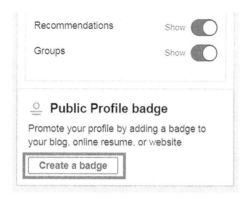

   To create a button that links to your LinkedIn profile, read LinkedIn's instructions for adding a profile badge to your blog, online resume or website. If you simply want to link one of the images on this page to your LinkedIn Profile, first copy and paste the badge that you like into your document (you might want to use your snipping tool).

If you choose to put a hyperlink into your resume, be aware that some recruiters' programs will strip out hyperlinks due to the possibility of viruses. So unless you're sending the resume to someone personally, include your full LinkedIn URL.

Results to Expect

Recruiters, employers and clients will have everything they need at their fingertips to get a full picture of who you are and what you offer. They will be ready, if they like what they see, to invite you to take the next step, whether that is submitting a resume or scheduling an interview or a meeting.

Bonus Tip #4

For Unemployed Job Seekers: What to Put in your Headline, Activity Updates and Experience Sections

Some of the most common questions I receive from job seekers are "What should I put in my headline?" "Should I put 'Seeking New Opportunities' in my Activity Updates?" "What should I put in my current Experience section if I'm not currently working?"

The Problem

We all know that despite the clear fact that unemployment does not truly indicate lack of talent or skill, many employers prefer to hire people who are currently employed. Ultimately, there will often be no perfect way to hide the fact that you are not currently working. However, there are many choices of how to approach this situation in your LinkedIn profile.

The Tune-Up

The biggest problem with figuring out how to handle unemployment is that there is no one right answer! What follows are some of my thoughts on how to approach each of three sections—Headline, Activity Update and Experience—as an unemployed job seeker.

Headline

Stock your headline with keywords relevant to your industry (see the very first section in this book). The most important thing you can do to appear in searches (in conjunction with expanding your network) is to have the right keywords in your profile. Whenever possible, also make your headline compelling with a unique selling proposition in order to increase interest once people find you (See **Mistake #1**). These are the most important factors in getting attention from recruiters and hiring managers.

In the past, some people have benefitted from putting "Seeking Opportunities" or "Open to New Opportunities" in their headline. Some recruiters used to search for the word "Opportunities" and approach people they knew are looking for a job. With the advent of Open Candidates, however, this strategy doesn't make sense anymore. Use the precious 120 characters in your headline for keywords and for conveying your USP (Unique Selling Proposition)!

Activity Updates and Interactivity

The most important thing you can do as a job seeker is to stay active on LinkedIn. Post industry-relevant articles and write them yourself if you can. Post comments on other valuable articles, especially on material relevant to your profession. Follow companies that interest you. Interact on the company pages of those companies. And apply to positions that you are qualified for.

I do not recommend posting anything about seeking opportunities in your activity updates. Instead, use this feature to write about what you're learning, what's inspiring you, and the success you're having in your life! Did you just get a new certification? An interview offer? Why not report that to the world? News like that will likely make you attractive to another organization. For more on how to post Activity Updates, see **Mistake #13**.

Open Candidates

As an unemployed job seeker, the good news is that there's no downside to letting the world know you're open to new opportunities. Go to the Job Seeking Preferences tab in your Settings & Privacy section, and turn on "Let recruiters know you're open to opportunities."

Let recruiters know you're open to opportunities   Close

Share that you're open and appear in recruiter searches matching your career
interests

Current Experience

Unemployed job seekers may approach this section in several ways. Following are some of the most common. Note that before changing your current job title, you should turn off your Activity Updates in your Privacy Settings. Be aware that when you change your current job title, LinkedIn will ask if this is your current title. Say "NO" to avoid having your headline replaced by the new title. You will be tempted to click "YES" but don't do it! This way your headline will remain the way you wrote it, with all the keywords you worked so hard to put in there (also see **Mistake #1**).

Here are some options for how to populate your current job title when you are not employed full time:

1. **"Consultant."** Some job seekers will create an Experience section that makes it look like they are a consultant. *Only do this if you are truly doing consulting work and can say something about it!* Otherwise it will look like you are hiding something. And always include keywords for what you are consulting about!

2. **"Manager, LinkedIn Group."** I do not recommend listing management of a LinkedIn group as a current job title, especially since the days of lucrative LinkedIn group empires seem to be long gone.

3. **"Job Title at Seeking Opportunities."** Some recruiters might respond negatively to this current experience description, and it won't help you since recruiters will recruit you if they like you, regardless of whether you are officially open to opportunities.

4. **Volunteer.** According to Link Humans, "42% of hiring managers surveyed by LinkedIn said they view volunteer experience as equivalent to formal work experience"! If you are participating significantly as a volunteer and have major accomplishments to report, putting a volunteer role in the current experience section may be appropriate. You don't necessarily need to specify that you are a volunteer—you can list your title and leave it at that. If the position is not worthy of the Experience section, use the Volunteer Experience section instead.

5. **Part-Time.** If you are employed part-time, there is absolutely no requirement that you reveal that fact. Complete the section as if the position were a full-time job. Enter the company name, your job title and accomplishments, and leave it at that.

6. **Parent.** If you are a stay-at-home mom or dad, you can list "Stay-at-Home Parent" as a job title; but if you were engaged in projects during that time, list those instead, with appropriate titles and descriptions.

7. **Blank.** This strategy is recommended by many recruiters. Their philosophy is that if you're not employed, honesty is the best policy.

The great thing about an online profile is that you can change it whenever you want and find out what works best for you. So you can try different ways of presenting yourself in your headline, summary, and job titles. Just remember to take control of your privacy settings when you make any changes.

Results to Expect

Being unemployed does not have to be a dealbreaker! If you stay active on LinkedIn and represent yourself as an experienced professional, you can attract the attention of recruiters and hiring managers.

Bonus Tip #5

Don't Violate LinkedIn's Terms of Service

LinkedIn's User Agreement is located at https://www.linkedin.com/legal/user-agreement.

The Problem

This document contains many rules and regulations that you might not be aware of, and that, if violated, could cause your account to be suspended or terminated. The section entitled "DO's and DON'Ts" is especially important to read. You might discover that you are violating one or more of the items on this list. You might also discover that another member is violating the user agreement.

Members are also not allowed to use workarounds for including contact information or keywords, such as putting a telephone number or other personal identification information in a field where there is no official field provided by LinkedIn for that purpose.

The Tune-Up

First of all, read LinkedIn's User Agreement![110] It's essential to be aware of all the terms of service that apply to you.

Do not include phone numbers or email addresses in your Headline. Do not include keywords in your Name field. Do not create more than one profile in the same language. Follow the rules!

Safeguard your login information so that no other parties can access your account. You can see all of the places you're currently logged in by going to Settings & Privacy and from the Account tab, clicking on "Where you're signed in."

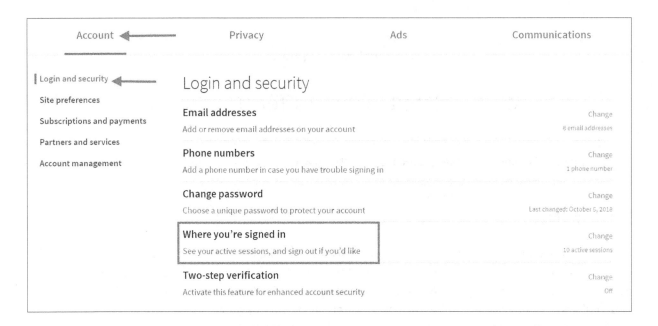

If you receive a notice that an unknown person attempted to log in or logged into your profile, change your password immediately!

As with any emails, do NOT click on any suspicious links in LinkedIn messages. They could be hackers. Here's an example of a spam message one of my connections received:

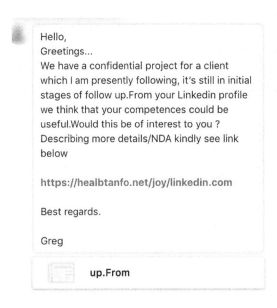

Unfortunately, my contact clicked on the link and the same message went out to all his connections. Two-step verification might have prevented this fiasco. Read this LinkedIn Help article[111] to learn how to turn on two-step verification.

What To Do If You Experience Hacking

If you experience any violations of LinkedIn's User Agreement or have questions about its terms, contact LinkedIn. Here's how:

Contact them online[112] or by physical mail.

For Members in the United States: LinkedIn Corporation
Attn: User Agreement Issues 2029 Stierlin Court Mountain View, CA 94043

For Members outside the United States: LinkedIn Ireland
Attn: User Agreement Issues
Gardner House, Wilton Place, Wilton Plaza
Dublin 2 94043 Ireland

There are, unfortunately, some inappropriate activities that LinkedIn will not address. If someone obtains your email address through your LinkedIn account and then sends you email outside of LinkedIn, there is nothing that LinkedIn will do about it—even if the person explicitly says they got your contact information from LinkedIn. So be careful about whom you connect with on LinkedIn!

Results to Expect

By understanding and abiding by LinkedIn's User Agreement, you'll retain your LinkedIn membership status so you can create relationships and produce results through LinkedIn for many years to come. And by protecting your account, as well as taking action if someone else violates the User Agreement, you will feel more secure and in control of your LinkedIn experience.

Bonus Tip #6

Hidden Search Tools

The Problem

With LinkedIn's constant updates sometimes comes the unfortunate loss of functions. The new interface change that happened in early 2017 left a few things wanting—but it also has some great new hidden features that might become a permanent part of the functionality of LinkedIn down the road. One of those is the external search of topics and titles.

The Tune-Up

Search by Industry-Specific Topic

Want to know more about a specific topic or connect with people and groups who know about a specific topic? Let's say the topic is "job search." Type https://www.linkedin.com/topic/job-search and LinkedIn will generate a list of names of people on LinkedIn with knowledge of job search, popular posts on the topic of job search, top presentations about job search, and LinkedIn groups about job search.

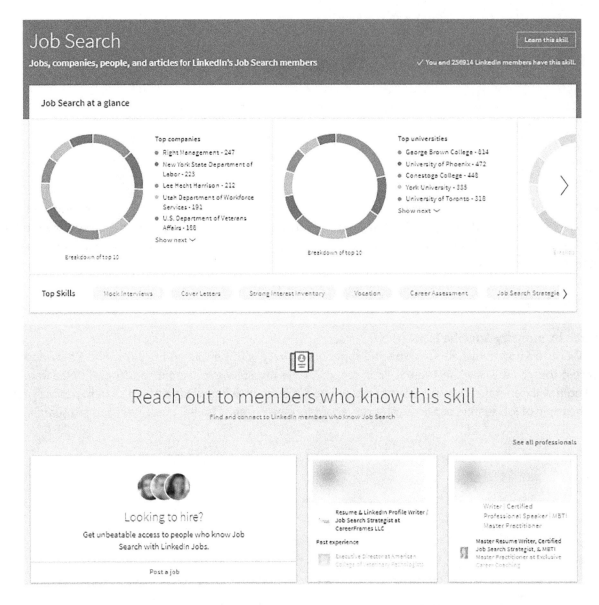

You can conduct this type of search for any topic! Just type this URL https://www.linkedin.com/topic/ followed by your keyword. If it's more than one word, use a space or a dash between words, such as job-search, interview-skills, lead generation strategies, etc. Be warned that you might get some advertising thrown at you if you type in a popular keyword phrase.

Search by Industry-Specific Title

If you're looking to connect, and want to find members according to their industry, use https://www.linkedin.com/title/ followed by the industry of your choice. For instance, if you're interested in becoming a graphic designer, enter https://www.linkedin.com/title/graphic-designer and you'll be rewarded with a cornucopia of information, such as how many LinkedIn members claim this skill, where they work and went to college, the names of professionals you can connect with, graphic design courses available through Lynda.com, top articles, and more!

Results to Expect

By using these "secret" URLs, you'll have easy, efficient access to people, information and trainings that other LinkedIn users might not even know exist. Taking advantage of tricks like this will make you a true LinkedIn power user.

Bonus Tip #7

Creating a Secondary Language Profile

The Problem

LinkedIn reports that 70% of its members are located outside of the US. Because such a large portion of users are multilingual and interested in connecting with people both inside and outside of English-speaking countries, I am including this special section on how to set up additional LinkedIn profiles that cater to secondary languages.

If you are multilingual, you probably have people searching for you in multiple languages. If you post your profile only in one of them, you could be losing the opportunity to connect with at least half your audience.

The Tune-Up

If you speak two languages and want people to find your profile in a second language, you can create a secondary language profile. To do this, go to your Profile page and click on "Add profile in another language" in the right sidebar:

Choose your language from the drop-down menu. LinkedIn supports the following languages as of October 2018:

English, Arabic, Bahasa Indonesia, Chinese (Simplified), Chinese (Traditional), Czech, Danish, Dutch, French, German, Italian, Japanese, Korean, Malay, Norwegian, Polish, Portuguese, Romanian, Russian, Spanish, Swedish, Tagalog, Thai, Turkish

> **Note:** You cannot change the default language of your profile once you've set it up in a particular language. It's recommended that you set up a secondary language profile instead.

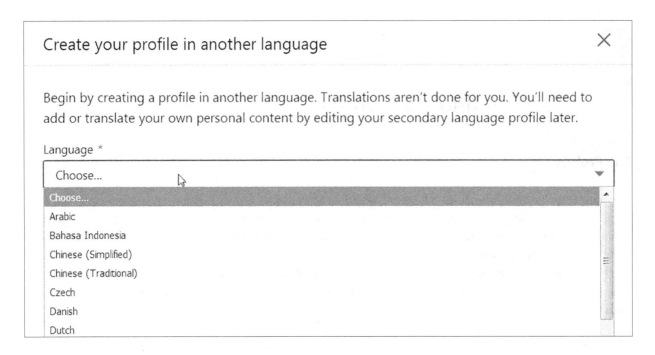

Be sure to update your name and Headline before clicking "Create Profile."

LinkedIn does not translate your content for you, so now you'll need to edit your secondary language profile. To do so, go to new language profile by selecting it from the upper right corner:

While viewing your secondary language profile, you can edit the Summary, Experience, and Education sections as you normally would. When you click the pencil icon to edit one of these sections, you'll see that LinkedIn provides a snapshot of your primary profile to help you:

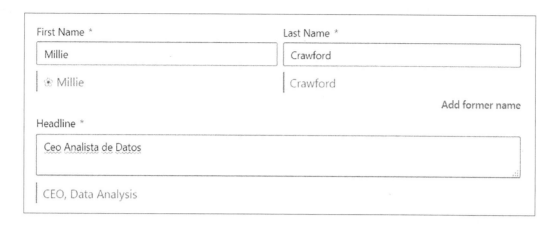

Note: Your Skills and Endorsements can't be edited and will only appear in the language of your primary profile. Recommendations will also only show in the language in which they were written.

When a member signs in to LinkedIn and views your profile, they will see it in the language of your primary account; or, if you have multiple profiles in several languages, viewers will see the one most relevant to them. The viewer has the ability to choose from your language profiles by selecting one from the upper right corner of your profile.

All of your language profiles will show up in search engines and have their own URL that includes "/?locale=" and the code for that language. For instance, a profile in French would appear as https://www.linkedin.com/in/yourname/?local=fr_FR.

If you no longer want your secondary language profile, you can delete it by selecting the language from your drop-down list and clicking the "x."

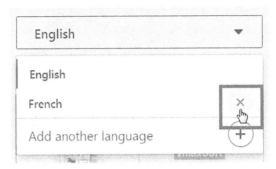

Note that when you make a post on your page or publish an article, regardless of the language, it will be connected with both your language profiles but will only be shown in the language in which it was written. So you might want to post things in multiple languages to reach multiple audiences and to appear in both newsfeeds and searches in multiple languages.

Results to Expect

Here's the good news: All of your language profiles will show up in search engines and have their own URL, searchable in Google. Plus, having multiple language profiles will make the user experience for your viewers a more fluid and positive one, since they will be able to explore who you are in their own language. You'll also be found for your skills in multiple languages when people search for someone like you on LinkedIn. So if you do business in more than one language, a secondary language profile is a must-have!

Insufficient or Ineffective Group Membership

LinkedIn groups are communities of individuals with similar interests or a professional common ground. There are groups for people who are job seekers (which also contain recruiters and employers); groups for people with particular technical knowledge; and groups for lawyers, project managers, graduates from various schools, and even cooks.

Once you join a group, you have access to Conversations and Job Postings relevant to that group, and you yourself can post discussions and answer questions asked in the group.

There are reportedly over 2 million groups on LinkedIn and on average, each user is a member of 7 groups. You can choose to join up to 100 LinkedIn groups.

There's a lot of buzz that LinkedIn groups are on the decline. Until they are eliminated, I don't think it's time to abandon ship. It's my opinion that the decline in activity may be due in part to LinkedIn's new, stricter rules regarding group participation and also because more discussions are beginning to take place on Publisher. Groups are still an effective tool to make connections and establish thought leadership.

The Problem

LinkedIn groups can provide you with access to thousands of potential readers. If you're not a member of groups relevant to you, you won't be reaching the targeted people you want to reach, and your networking opportunities will be limited.

As business consultant Laurie Phillips states, "Group memberships and activity gives me a clue about whether the candidate is building a broad business network, as well as what topics/organizations they associate with closely. It's a great source for insight on someone before I meet with them."

The Tune-Up

Search for and join groups where you will connect with your target audience. For instance, if you are seeking a job in the IT industry, join IT-related groups and job-seeking groups such as Linked:HR that contain recruiters. If you provide services to small businesses, join groups such as the Small Business Forum. If you provide services to children, join groups that contain parents. You will then have access to the people you want to reach.

There are several ways to find groups to join:

1. Conduct a search.

To find groups that might interest you on LinkedIn, In the search box, type the search terms that are relevant to you, and a link for groups with that topic will come up. If you type "Project Manager" into the search bar, then select "Groups" from the drop-down menu . . .

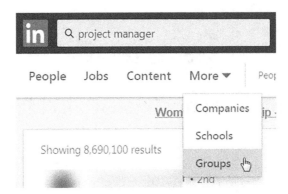

. . . you'll be taken to a list of groups that you can join. Or, access this page by clicking on the magnifying glass in a blank search bar. On the search page, select the "Groups" tab and type in your search terms above:

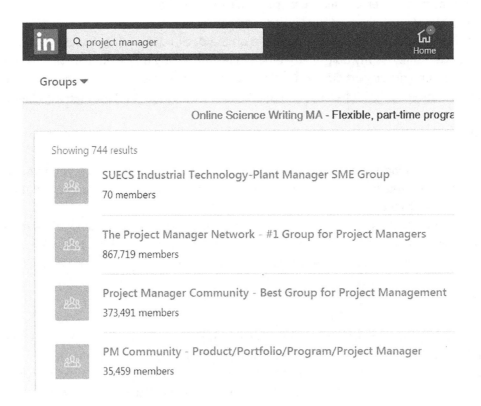

You can also select "People" from the drop-down while you're there and find out what groups they belong to. See my next point below!

2. Join groups based on who is in them.

Are there people you particularly respect on LinkedIn? Perhaps they are members of groups you would want to belong to. When you view someone's profile, you can view their group membership, unless they have hidden this information.

To do so, scroll down to the bottom of their profile, where you'll see a block of people, companies, groups and schools they are following. To view just the groups, click on the "See all" link:

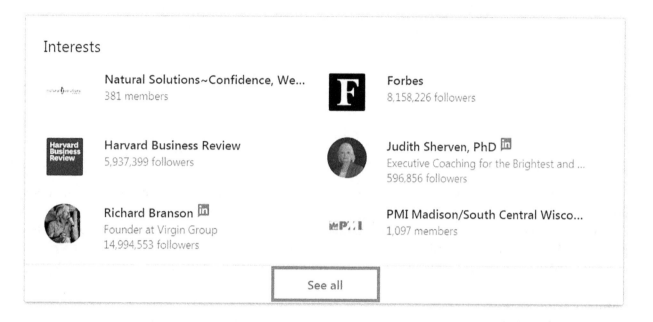

Then select the Groups tab and click on the name of the group(s) you are interested in joining.

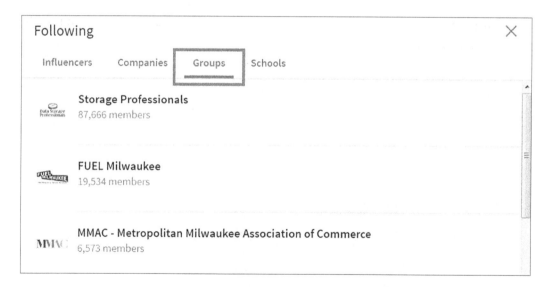

Post to groups

To start a conversation, go to your groups page and click on the group you'd like to engage.

Click on "Start a new conversation in this group," add a captivating introduction, and then enter any details you'd like.

Best practice is to enter a true conversation starter that will engage your audience. If you put spammy marketing material into the details section, you will likely be chastised with a warning from the group moderator. Make sure you're following group rules before posting anything to any group!

Posting Videos

LinkedIn has improved the sharing experience in groups and article posts by allowing videos.

To post a video in a group, "Start a new conversation in this group" by clicking in the details field and pasting in the URL of the video. You may need to add a space after pasting in the URL to see the video populate the preview field below. Once the preview is in place, you can delete the ugly URL and give your post a title and further details if you like.

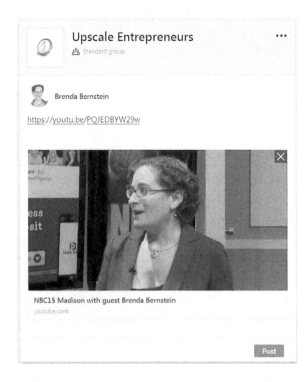

Or, click on the video camera icon to attach a video file up to 10 minutes long from your computer.

Your video will look like a player at first, but once you hit post and the video is fully uploaded, it will look more like this:

General advice on joining and participating in groups:

Before joining a group, check the number of members. Ideally, you will join a mix of groups, some with membership in the thousands and some smaller ones. Groups with only a few hundred members might get you more attention if you post something, since there are not as many people posting. I have personally found the members of local groups tend to respond more often to my posts than people in bigger groups with wider membership.

There are hundreds of thousands of members in many groups! If you're looking to greatly expand your network, you might want to join one of these mammoth connector groups (LION is one of them) and start making invitations.

To join a group, just click "Join." You will either be automatically accepted into the group, or your request will go to a moderator who will approve or deny your request. Most of the time you will be approved.

Once you join a group, don't just sit there . . . do something!

Use Conversations to share articles relevant to your groups. Start discussions that the group will find interesting. Share images. Respond to other people's comments. Post news articles. Put yourself out there. Then let the group take your conversations and run with them.

You can hover over a person's name within a group discussion to find out more about them. If you like what they said and see value in having them in your network, send them a customized invitation! After you have connected, you can mention them in a group conversation using the @ symbol. This is an effective way to make long-lasting connections and maybe even get some help with an issue you're facing. I recommend setting up a phone call or coffee date to really get to know the people in your group who could be valuable connections.

> **HINT:** When you share group membership with someone, you can send them a message without being connected. To message a group member, click on the number of members in the upper right-hand corner of the group page.

Hovering just to the right of the listing will reveal an envelope icon. Click it and send your message.

If a member has caught your attention with an interesting post, you can message them by clicking on their name and messaging them directly.

BIG HINT: If you're looking to stand out and be noticed on LinkedIn, prioritize participating in conversations where there are already a LOT of comments—over 100 at least. Most of those people will be following the discussion and will therefore get an email when a new comment is posted. That means they will read your comment—and if you impress them, they might soon be asking you for help!

Participation gets you noticed. If your goal is effective networking, your participation, more than how many groups you've joined, is what's important.

Note: If you are a member of a group but don't want the public to know for any reason, you can hide the groups in your list. To do this, click on the three dots in the upper right of the group's feed and select "Update your settings".

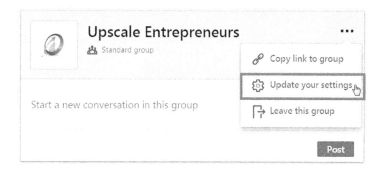

To hide the group, switch the "Display group on profile" option to No.

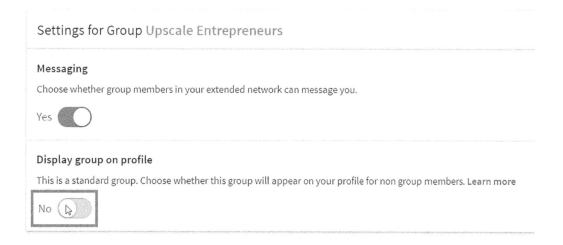

As of January 2019, LinkedIn does not provide any email notifications for group discussion/ activity. However, the group notification is visible on the "Notifications" tab on the Homepage. When and if LinkedIn reinstates group email notifications, I recommend opting for weekly digests, since the email traffic can be heavy! Or you can also choose not to receive updates from certain groups if you are feeling overwhelmed by the volume of email you are receiving.

Results to Expect

The results you get from group participation are what you make them. If you participate in active discussions, you will gain visibility. If you use groups to find valuable connections and build your network, you will get the value they offer. And when and if LinkedIn restores some of the functionality in Groups, you'll be in a great position to hit the ground running.

Appendix A

LinkedIn Profile Completion Checklist

Use this checklist to assess and update your LinkedIn profile based on the tips in this book. You can also download and print this checklist.[113]

- ◯ My profile uses highly searched keywords and an informative headline.
- ◯ My photo is a professional, closely cropped "head shot."
- ◯ My contact information is complete, including my website URLs.
- ◯ I have a custom URL for my public profile (possibly with keywords included).
- ◯ I have at least 500 connections.
- ◯ My profile contains a compelling summary section.
- ◯ My job duties and accomplishments are described in clear, concrete language.
- ◯ My profile is formatted consistently and is free of spelling, grammar, and punctuation errors.
- ◯ My profile is formatted attractively.
- ◯ I have completed the Skills section and chosen my top three.
- ◯ I have endorsements for my most essential skills.
- ◯ I have taken advantage of Special Sections to provide additional detail about my accomplishments.
- ◯ I have attached media items in my Summary and Experience Sections.
- ◯ I have used the Jobs function on LinkedIn (if you are a job seeker or employer).
- ◯ I have at least three (and preferably 10), well-written recommendations.
- ◯ I review my LinkedIn profile at least monthly, and update it when needed.
- ◯ I have exported and saved a backup copy of my profile in .pdf format.
- ◯ If I own a business, I have created a Company page.
- ◯ I use my LinkedIn profile URL in my email signature and on my resume.
- ◯ If I am unemployed, my Headline, Activity Updates and Experience sections contain appropriate information.
- ◯ If I am bilingual, I have created a Secondary Language Profile.
- ◯ I am in full compliance with LinkedIn's Terms of Service.

Total Completed: _____

Notes:

Appendix B

Character Limits for your LinkedIn Profile Sections

When writing your LinkedIn profile sections, it is helpful to know the character limits you are working with! Here are some of the most important character limits to know that will help you plan your work and work your plan on LinkedIn:

The Basics

First name: 20 characters
Last name: 40 characters
Maiden name: 40 characters
URL: 5 to 29 characters following "linkedin.com/in/"

Main Profile Sections

Professional Headline: 120 characters Summary: 2,000 characters
Company Name: 100 characters
Job Title (in Experience section): 100 characters
Description (in Experience section): 2,000 characters
Activities and Societies (in Education): 500 characters
Education Description: 1,000 characters
Education/Degree: 100 characters
Honors & Awards: 1,000 characters
Skills: 80 characters each (up to 50 skills)
Recommendations: 3,000 characters

Contact & Personal Information

Website Anchor Text: 30 characters
Website URL: 256 characters
Address: 1,000 characters (visible only 1st degree connections)
Phone: 25 characters
Personal Info-Instant messenger: 25 characters

Activity and Publishing

Activity update: 700 characters (only 140 will transfer to Twitter)
Publisher Post Headline: 150 characters
Publisher Post Content: 40,000 characters

Connections & Invitations

Number of direct, first-level connections: 30,000

Company Pages

Section	Field	Character Limit
Page tab	Company Update text	1300
Page tab	Company Name	100
Page tab	About Us	2000
Career Pages - Life tab	Page Name	50
Career Pages - Life tab	Company Leaders headline	150
Career Pages - Life tab	Company Leaders description	150
Career Pages - Life tab	Employee Testimonials	400
Career Pages - Life tab	Custom Module title	150
Career Pages - Life tab	Custom Module body	500
Career Pages - Life tab	Custom Module URL label	70

Groups

Group Discussion Title: 200 characters
Group Discussion Body: 1,300 characters
Group Discussion Comments: 1,250 characters
Profile 'Publication' Title: 255 characters
Profile 'Publication' Description: 2,000 characters
Maximum number of groups: 100
Maximum number of pending groups: 20
Maximum groups managed by one individual: 30
Number of mentions you can use in one group conversation: 20
Number of owners a group can have: 1
Number of managers a group can have: 20
Maximum number of members in each group: 20,000

For more group-related limits, read General Limits for LinkedIn Groups.[114]

Appendix C

LinkedIn Image Dimensions

All LinkedIn images can be uploaded in PNG, JPEG/JPG or GIF formats.

Profile Photo

The maximum size of a LinkedIn profile photo is 8MB. The image must be between 200 x 200 and 500 x 500 (ideally 400 x 400).

Background Photo

Maximum size is 8MB. Recommended pixel dimensions are 1584 x 396px.

Company & Career Pages

The following chart is borrowed from LinkedIn Help:

Tab	Module	Minimum Image Size	Recommended Image Size
Page Tab	Logo Image	300 (w) x 300 (h) pixels	300 (w) x 300 (h) pixels
Page Tab	Overview Tab Image	360 (w) x 120 (h) pixels	360 (w) x 120 (h) pixels
Page Tab	Cover Image	1192 (w) x 220 (h) pixels	1536 (w) x 768 (h) pixels
Life Tab	Hero Image	1128 (w) x 376 (h) pixels	1128 (w) x 376 (h) pixels
Life Tab	Custom Modules	502 (w) x 282 (h) pixels	502 (w) x 282 (h) pixels
Life Tab	Company Photos	264 (w) x 176 (h) pixels	900 (w) x 600 (h) pixels

Note that Career Pages are a paid feature. To learn more, read LinkedIn Career Pages - Overview.[115]

Appendix D

LinkedIn's 25 Hottest Skills & Overused Buzzwords

LinkedIn's 25 Hottest Skills

Each year, LinkedIn publishes the 25 "hottest" skills that get people hired. If you have this year's skills, you may have been on the radar of several hiring companies.

Below is LinkedIn's 2017 list. Depicted here are what LinkedIn deems the most sought-after skills by recruiters all over the world. If you're interested in a breakdown of related courses and job openings based on this list, see the LinkedIn® Blog original article, The Skills Companies Need Most in 2018 – And The Courses to Get Them.[116]

In a computer and nanotech-driven world, it's no surprise that the hottest skills right now are in the technical realm.

Hard Skills

1. Cloud and Distributed Computing
2. Statistical Analysis and Data Mining
3. Middleware and Integration Software
4. Web Architecture and Development Framework
5. User Interface Design
6. Software Revision Control Systems
7. Data Presentation
8. SEO/SEM Marketing
9. Mobile Development
10. Network and Information Security
11. Marketing Campaign Management
12. Data Engineering and Data Warehousing
13. Storage Systems and Management
14. Electronic and Electrical Engineering
15. Algorithm Design
16. Perl/Python/Ruby
17. Shell Scripting Languages
18. Mac, Linux and Unix Systems
19. Java Development

20. Business Intelligence

21. Software QA and User Testing

22. Virtualization

23. Automotive Services, Parts and Design

24. Economics

25. Database Management and Software

Do you need to add some of these skill sets to your LinkedIn® profile? See **Mistake #12** for tips on how to do that.

LinkedIn's Overused Buzzwords

LinkedIn also intermittently provides a list of overused professional buzzwords for the year. Here are the top offenders for you to avoid, published in LinkedIn's official SlideShare presentation, You're Better Than Buzzwords — Start Showing It.[117]

1. Specialized (new this year!)

2. Leadership (dropped from #1)

3. Passionate (up from the #4 spot)

4. Strategic (up from the #5 spot)

5. Experienced (new!)

6. Focused (new!)

7. Expert (back on the list after being #10 in 2014)

8. Certified (new!)

9. Creative (down after holding at #3 for two years)

10. Excellent (new!)

Words like "innovative" and "analytical" have disappeared from the list this year, but if buzzword history shows us anything, they will be back! And, frankly, some of those words are "overused" because they work! Before you jump on the bandwagon and re-wordsmith everything in your profile, read my article, LinkedIn's Overused Buzzwords for 2017 – Do You Really Need to Avoid Them?[118]

The Essay Expert's writers can work with you to write a profile that stands out from the rest of the world's. For details on our services see LinkedIn Profile Writing Services.[119] You can also contact us through our web form.[120] We look forward to giving you that extra edge on LinkedIn!

Appendix E

LinkedIn For Students

Calling all 40 million student members: Did you know that LinkedIn has resources tailored just for you?

LinkedIn Higher Education[121] is filled with videos and tips on the most effective ways to use LinkedIn, from building your personal brand to getting an internship.

- Available videos cover a variety of topics to get you started with networking, discovering your career passion, and prepping for interviews. You'll also find checklists and tip sheets for building your student profile and utilizing LinkedIn's Alumni tools.

- The Student Job Hunting Handbook Series[122] provides tips for optimizing your LinkedIn® profile, approaching the college job hunt, and applying for internships and entry-level positions.

- LinkedIn Student Careers[123] is LinkedIn's search engine for internship positions and jobs for recent graduates. Search by industry for a list of positions that may interest you.

- LinkedIn for Students Articles[124] contains a collection of articles written by LinkedIn's top writers related to college and career.

Add to Profile

LinkedIn's Add to Profile[125] feature will make adding your degrees and certification to your LinkedIn Profile a breeze. Released to colleges and universities in March 2015, "educational institutions can embed a simple link on their websites and in emails sent directly to graduates. When graduates click the "Add to Profile" button, they'll have the option to add that achievement directly to the "Education" section of their LinkedIn profile by previewing it and hitting Save."

For more information on this feature read the LinkedIn Blog article, LinkedIn Opens Up Profiles to Higher Education Partners with One-Click Program.[126]

Appendix F

Information on Paid Accounts

A survey by Statista[127] found that 79% of LinkedIn users use the free account; only 20% of those surveyed paid to use LinkedIn.

While a large proportion of paid subscribers are recruiters, many others who value the paid features of LinkedIn are signing up for premium accounts. If you want to promote your services on LinkedIn Profinder, you'll need a premium account. Or, if the ability to send InMail, view more information about who viewed your profile, and organize your contacts is worth a bit extra, you might want to upgrade.

LinkedIn frequently offers free month-long trials, which you can take advantage of before paying for features you're not sure you'll need.

For more information, go to these links:

LinkedIn® Free and Premium Accounts[128]

LinkedIn® Premium Business[129]

LinkedIn® Premium Career[130]

LinkedIn Talent Solutions[131]

LinkedIn® Sales Solutions / Sales Navigator[132]

Appendix G

Get Free E-Book Updates

Kindle Version

Amazon provides published updates as follows:

1. Major Updates

If Amazon considers an e-book update to be "critical," they will send a notification email to all customers who purchased the e-book. You will be able to opt in to receive the update through the Manage Your Content and Devices page on Amazon.com.

Whenever there is a "major" change to a book, Amazon will update it for free. Just make sure your "Automatic Book Update" is turned on. Here's how:

- Log in to your Amazon account and go to Your Content and Devices page. You can also access this by selecting it from the "Accounts & Lists" drop-down menu.

- Go to the Preferences tab, scroll down to "Automatic Book Updates" and make sure the switch is set to ON.

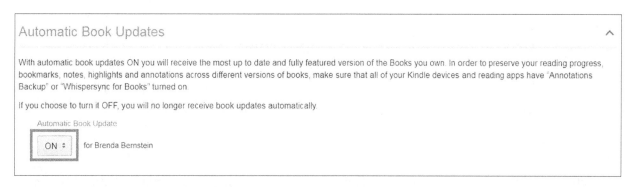

- You should then receive a notice whenever an updated version of the book is available, which you will be able access via your Manage Your Content and Devices page.

If you do not receive a notice, it's possible you missed it; simply log in to your Manage Your Content and Devices page and check to see if the new version is there. If it isn't, you may want to contact Amazon directly to find out why.

When a new edition of *How to Write a KILLER LinkedIn Profile* is available, you'll see "Update Available" next to the title.

Select the checkbox to the left of the title and you'll see that the "Deliver" button becomes live.

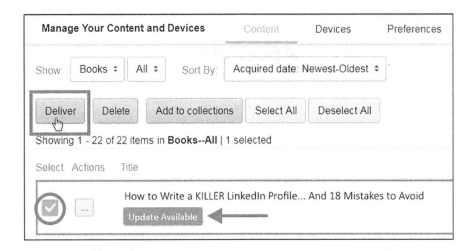

Click on the Deliver button and in the pop-up window, select your device and hit Deliver again.

2. Minor Updates

If changes to the content are considered minor by Amazon, customers will not be notified by email; however, Amazon will still activate your ability to update the content through the Manage Your Content and Devices on Amazon.com.

If you would like to be alerted by The Essay Expert when there are future revisions to the Kindle edition, you can sign up here.[133]

Appendix H

Settings & Privacy

Accessing Your Settings and Privacy

I've referred to many privacy settings throughout this book, and since many people are not aware of many of the settings, or have questions about where to find them, it's worth devoting a section to this important topic. You have control over many aspects of your LinkedIn profile you might not even know about! It's all in the Settings & Privacy portal.

To access Settings & Privacy, click on your profile image thumbnail in the upper right of your account and select "Settings & Privacy" from the drop-down menu. Once there, a whole world of options will open up to you! Here's a breakdown of the most important things you can do to take control over what's visible and accessible in your LinkedIn profile. It's not a complete list—because that would be a very long list—but I think you'll find a lot of goodies here.

Account Tab

Login and security

- Email addresses: Add and remove email addresses and designate your primary email where you'll receive all of your notifications.

- Phone numbers: Add a recovery phone number just in case you ever have trouble signing in.

- Where you're signed in: Review and close locations where you—or someone else—logged in and never logged out.

Site preferences

- Language: Choose the language you use to view LinkedIn (this does not change the language with which you created your profile).

- Autoplay videos: Choose if you want videos to autoplay on your browser.

- Showing profile photos: Choose whether to hide your profile photos or show them to everyone on LinkedIn, just your network, or just your connections.

Partners and services

- Microsoft: View Microsoft accounts you've connected to your LinkedIn account.

- Permitted Services: See a list of services (except Twitter) you've authorized to access your LinkedIn account and remove them.

- Twitter settings: Add and remove Twitter access to your LinkedIn account.

Account management

- Merging LinkedIn accounts: Provide the username and password of an account that you want to transfer connections from, then close it (this does not merge profile information).

- Closing your LinkedIn account: Find out what you might need to do before closing your account, then close it.

> **Note:** You might need to contact LinkedIn Help to merge or close your account. Many people have reported challenges when attempting to get this done.

Privacy Tab

How others see your profile and network information

- Edit your public profile: A quick link to your public profile settings, including editing your URL, content, visibility, and more.

- Who can see your email address: Choose whether to allow connections to download your email and if whether to hide your email from connections altogether or make it visible to all or part of your network. If you want recruiters to contact you, I recommend having your email address visible to everyone, and/or including it in your Summary section.

- Who can see your connections: Prevent your 1st degree connections from seeing exactly how many connections you have and who those connections are.

- Who can see your last name: Choose between your full surname or first initial.

- Representing your organization and interests: Select whether LinkedIn should mention you on job postings or company page insights of your employers or any company you show public interest in. If you're a stealth job seeker, you probably want this setting turned off!

- Profile visibility off LinkedIn: Choose whether to show information from your profile to users of permitted services such as Outlook.

- Microsoft Word: Choose whether work experience descriptions from your LinkedIn profile can be shown in Resume Assistant. See my article, LinkedIn + Microsoft's Resume Assistant: Friend or Foe?[134]

How others see your LinkedIn activity

- Profile viewing options: Choose whether you want to appear as you or an anonymous member when viewing someone else's profile.

- Manage active status: Choose whether you want everyone, just your connections, or no one to see that you're logged into your account.

- Share job changes, education changes, and work anniversaries from profile: Choose whether you want your network notified when you make a change to your profile. Why job changes and work anniversaries are in the same category, I don't know. But for now, they come together.

- Notifying connections when you're in the news: Choose whether to notify connections when you've been @mentioned. I highly recommend turning this one on!

- Mentions or tags by others: Choose whether members can @mention or tag you. I also recommend turning this on if you want publicity at all!

How LinkedIn uses your data

- Manage your data and activity: See a history of changes you've made to your account and manage those changes.

- Download your data: Download an archive of your account data, posts, connections, and more.

- Manage who can discover your profile from your email address: Exactly what it says.

- Manage who can discover your profile from your phone number: Ditto.

- Sync calendar: Sync your online calendar and to get meeting reminders and updates from your LinkedIn mobile app (learn more).[135]

- Salary data on LinkedIn: View and delete your salary data.

- Personal demographic information: Choose what details you provide about your gender, race, disability, and veteran status.

- Social, economic and workplace research: Choose whether LinkedIn can share your data with 3rd-party services.

Job seeking preferences

- Job application settings: Choose whether LinkedIn can save the information you provide in your job applications.

- Let recruiters know you're open to opportunities: Choose to let recruiters know you're open to opportunities and appear in their searches.

- Signal your interest to recruiters at companies you have created job alerts for: Allow recruiters for companies you're interested in to see your interest and also manage your job alerts.

- Sharing your profile when you click apply: Choose if you want to share your full profile with LinkedIn job posters whose applications are hosted off LinkedIn.

Blocking and hiding

- Followers: Choose whether everyone or just 1st-tier connections can follow you and see your public updates.

- Blocking: See your list of blocked members and unblock as desired.

Ads Tab

General advertising preferences

- Profile data for ad personalization: Control how certain ads appear to you.

Data collected on LinkedIn

- In multiple categories, control whether LinkedIn can use data about you to show more relevant jobs and ads based on your and similar members' information on LinkedIn. You might not want LinkedIn to use this information for privacy reasons, but if you turn these off, you'll still get ads—just less relevant ones.

Third party data

- Same as above, based on your interactions with businesses and other ad-related actions.

Communications Tab

Channels

- Notifications on LinkedIn: Manage the alerts you receive in the Notifications tab.
- Email frequency: Choose what types of emails you wish to receive from LinkedIn and whether you'd like to receive them as they occur or as a weekly digest.
- SMS frequency: Choose whether you would like to receive text notifications regarding new job opportunities or when a recruiter sends an InMail.

Preferences

- Who can send you invitations: Did you even know you could control this?
- Messages from members and partners: Choose whether you'd like to receive InMail,[136] Open Profile[137] messages or Sponsored InMail.[138]
- Read receipts and typing indicators: Choose whether you want the connection your messaging to that you are typing and that their messages have been read.
- Messaging reply suggestions: Choose whether you'd like LinkedIn to recommend replies when responding to a message. Personally, I like having some options—it's efficient. And I think LinkedIn is getting better with their suggestions.

Groups

- Group invitations: Choose whether you want to receive invitations to join groups.

LinkedIn messages

- Participate in research: Choose whether you'd like to receive invitations to participate in research on LinkedIn.

I hope at least a few of the above items were good news for you and that you feel more confident in the control you have over your LinkedIn profile.

Appendix I

Recommended Resources

Need LinkedIn Technical Help?

From time to time, you might encounter technical questions about how LinkedIn works, or LinkedIn might change something unexpectedly. For those sticky situations, I recommend contacting LinkedIn® Help.[139]

There is also a public forum for LinkedIn-related help topics.[140] LinkedIn offers these discussion tips for posting in the help forum:

1. Forum discussions are public. Please don't write anything you don't want the world to see, such as passwords, phone numbers, and email addresses.

2. Before you post, search for similar existing discussions that might help.

3. Include any details that will help others respond to your question.

4. Add tags that will help other members find your discussion.

Are You a Job Seeker?

LinkedIn has still not eliminated the need for a static resume! To that end, I've written 2 resume do-it-yourself books. These easy-to-read, practical and up-to-date guides will take you through the resume writing process step by step, from thinking through your approach to creating a great format, crafting effective branding statements and bullets, and handling specific challenges.

Available on Amazon:

How to Write a WINNING Resume . . . 50 Tips to Reach Your Job Search Target
Kindle: $6.97 US

"Brenda's book provides the serious kick a jobseeker needs to get motivated and keep moving. The book includes lots of resources—so many, in fact, that I stopped reading on my Kindle and moved to my PC reader so that I could get a better look at all the material provided."

— JoAnne Goldberg, Stanford MBA

"Bernstein's guide was incredibly useful in helping me to understand how I could deviate from the white-bread chronological resume to best highlight and illustrate the skills I had developed in that time that would be of interest to an employer. The end result is that I actually got the first job for which I applied, one that many people may have considered a bit of a reach for an individual returning to a career path from which he deviated nearly a decade ago."

— Ryan G., Madison, WI

"I was struggling to update my resume after letting it go stale for a few years before I contacted Brenda. Within a few weeks of updating it as well as my LinkedIn profile, I was contacted for an interview."

— J. Jung, Senior Systems Analyst, Irvine, CA

How to Write a STELLAR Executive Resume . . . 50 Tips to Reach Your Job Search Target

Kindle: $8.01 US   Print: $12.23 US

"If you put Brenda's easy-to-follow tips and guidelines into action, you will, without a doubt, set your resume apart from the competition. Brenda's 'can do' suggestions are sure to kick both the substance and format of your résumé up a notch, or two, or ten!"

— Posey Salem, Professional Resume Writer and Certified Instructional Systems Designer, Jacksonville, NC

"Brenda offers tips galore, covers new technology, and includes links to more resources! I will be strongly suggesting that my own Executive level clients consider adding this amazing resource to their library. Well done!"

— Stephanie Clark, Master Resume Writer and Master Certified Resume Strategist, Canada

---

Click here to get free excerpts of both of these books![141]

Just having a great resume and LinkedIn profile is not enough. You need to know how to use them! To that end, I've partnered with Mary Elizabeth Bradford to offer a trusted and award-winning resource, The Job Search Success System.[142]

Save yourself the cost of a job search coach with this proven 10-step system!

Free Webinar and Podcast Recordings

I've hosted multiple webinars and made guest appearances on several radio shows on the topic of LinkedIn, job search, resume writing and more. See The Essay Expert's Webinars & Podcasts page[143] for recordings and upcoming events.

Free Bi-Weekly LinkedIn Tips Right in Your Inbox

Subscribe to The Essay Expert's LinkedIn & Professional Writing e-list[144] to receive helpful emails that include news, tips and tricks on how to best utilize LinkedIn.

Appendix J

Important Opportunities to Give and Receive

Get Free Updates Until the Next Big Release

LinkedIn is constantly changing, and I will be issuing small revisions to this book throughout the year until the release of my new product.

- For PDF version owners: You will automatically receive the latest revisions to *How to Write a KILLER LinkedIn Profile* when they become available.
- For Kindle version owners: Amazon only notifies book owners that an updated version is available when they consider the changes to be "significant." Sign up here[145] and we'll be happy to give you a heads up if a new Kindle edition becomes available.

  Here's the easiest way to get PDF updates hassle-free: Just email us at TEESupport@TheEssayExpert.com with a copy of your receipt and we'll be happy to add you to our list to get all future KILLER updates automatically!

Want to see the answer to your LinkedIn question featured in the next edition of this book?

If you have a question regarding LinkedIn that you would like to see covered in the next edition, please email TEESupport@TheEssayExpert.com with your suggestion. The answer to your question might be featured in the next edition of *How to Write a KILLER LinkedIn Profile*.

We Want Your Feedback!

We hope you've enjoyed *How to Write a KILLER LinkedIn Profile*! Did you find this book helpful? Please share a review on Amazon and let others know about the value you received.

Post a Review on Amazon!

Check Out Our Services

If you are still stuck on how to write your LinkedIn profile or your resume, consider The Essay Expert's LinkedIn or Resume Writing services. Contact us at TEESupport@TheEssayExpert.com or through our web form,[146] or call/text us at 718-390-6696. We look forward to working with you. Book purchasers receive special discounts on LinkedIn services from The Essay Expert. See **Appendix K** for **coupon codes** you can use right now.

Contact us at https://theessayexpert.com/contact/

Get on My Lists

Want news and updates from The Essay Expert? Sign up for my Weekly Blog at https://theessayexpert.com/subscribe-to-the-weekly-blog/. You will receive a free e-book preview that you can give to a friend!

Connect with The Essay Expert on Facebook

"Like" our Facebook Fan page now to connect with other readers and additional resources . . .

KILLER LinkedIn Profile Facebook Fan Page: https://www.facebook.com/linkedinprofiletips

And of course, please Connect with me on LinkedIn!

Appendix K

Discounted LinkedIn Services from The Essay Expert

If you're still struggling with what to write about yourself, it's time to stop!

You might wish to work with The Essay Expert directly. If so, we have discounts available for you on our LinkedIn packages. To take advantage of these offers, go to our LinkedIn Profile Writing page,[147] order one of the following packages, and enter the coupon code.

Feel free to start with this amazing offer:

$100 LinkedIn Profile Review Special — We'll begin with a questionnaire to help us get a better idea of your goals, target audience and professional background. Then Brenda will personally read through your profile to get a sense of what could be improved. She will follow up with a 15-minute phone conversation to answer your questions and advise you on the best direction for your LinkedIn profile! And if you decide to purchase a full package after that, you'll get $75 toward your purchase. It's a WIN-WIN!

Or, save yourself time and hassle with our full-service LinkedIn packages, using these codes:

SUCCESS150 ($150 Discount)
• Executive Resume + LinkedIn Profile Success Package

LINKEDIN150 ($150 Discount)
• Executive LinkedIn Profile Complete

SUCCESS100 ($100 Discount)
• Mid-Level Resume + LinkedIn Profile Success Package

LINKEDIN100 ($100 Discount)
• Mid-Level LinkedIn Profile Complete
• Executive LinkedIn Headline & Summary Special

LINKEDIN75 ($75 Discount)
• Mid-Level LinkedIn Headline & Summary Special

Here's what people are saying about The Essay Expert's LinkedIn Services:

"Compliments to Brenda and her team for delivering a product that exceeded my expectations. The whole transaction from order to acknowledgment, scheduling and follow through, was delivered as promised in a very personable and professional manner. Well worth the investment made."

— Linda Batista, PMP, Finance Manager, Dallas/Fort Worth Area

---

"Brenda did a fabulous job reviewing my LinkedIn profile. It was well worth the investment and I highly recommend her service. I received a detailed explanation and edits for each category, all the way down to recommendations. I feel much more confident in my LinkedIn profile after Brenda's review. Thanks for a job well done!"

— William L. Mitchell, IT Consultant, Greater New York City Area

---

"I found the response time to be very quick, the quality of work to be excellent, and the creativity of the suggestions to be superb. I believe the value I received from the review significantly exceeds the amount that I paid for the service. You must try it!"

— Mike Robar, Director of Mortgage Operations, Greater Philadelphia Area

---

"The engagement exceeded expectations—from the immediate reply to me here in China, to on-time turnaround, to The Essay Expert's ability to understand my needs. Thank you very much. Highly recommended!"

— Roger McDonald, Deputy Managing Director, Newport, UK

"The best investment I've made in my search efforts! Thank you!"
— David McKnight, President at Digital Publishing Innovation, Madison, WI

"As a result of my LinkedIn profile changes, I have had 17 requests made of me to meet with various potential clients and partners!"

— Aaron W., Business Consultant, Madison, WI

"My new profile meets my goals of a 'Killer profile'—and the process was done quickly, concisely, professionally. Nice job."

— Jim Masloski, Customs Brokerage Professional, Sioux Falls, SD

"[Brenda] provided thorough feedback on my LinkedIn profile, immediately increasing exposure, and leading to one new interview offer per week since that time. Amazing . . . truly amazing!!"
— Brian Hobbs, Asia/Middle East Security Specialist, Washington, DC

"My LinkedIn Summary 'sounds' great! I am so happy about what you have put together (and so relieved). I kept 'hitting the wall' when I tried to do it. I am very thrilled. Thank you!"
— Susan LePre, Public Health PhD, New York, NY

Thank you!

Here's to your success as you craft a KILLER LinkedIn Profile!

Reference Links

1 https://theundercoverrecruiter.com/linkedin-recruitment

2 https://www.statista.com/chart/17535/linkedin-profile-boosts-job-chances/

3 https://www.linkedin.com/legal/user-agreement

4 https://university.linkedin.com

5 https://blog.linkedin.com/2014/02/21/high-school-students-embrace-your-skills-show-your-professional-side-and-create-a-linkedin-profile?utm_source=feedburner&utm_medium=email&utm_campaign=Feed%3A+typepad%2Flinkedinblog+%28LinkedIn+Blog%29

6 https://www.cnbc.com/2017/12/27/7-linkedin-hacks-to-boost-your-chances-of-getting-a-new-job-in-2018.html

7 https://blog.linkedin.com

8 https://blog.linkedin.com/author/sabrina-johnson

9 https://blog.linkedin.com/2014/03/04/my-secret-career-weapon linkedin?utm_source=feedburner&utm_medium=email&utm_campaign=Feed%3A+typepad%2Flinkedinblog+%28LinkedIn+Blog%29

10 https://www.omnicoreagency.com/linkedin-statistics/

11 https://www.truconversion.com/blog/social-media/how-to-create-a-perfect-linkedin-profile/

12 https://www.linkedin.com/help/linkedin/answer/4447

13 https://www.linkedin.com/help/linkedin/answer/6545?lang=en

14 https://mashable.com/2012/08/02/higher-google-search-results/

15 https://theessayexpert.com/contact/

16 https://theessayexpert.com/linkedin-profiles/

17 https://blog.linkedin.com/2016/05/25/get-comfortable-with-being-uncomfortable-why-now-is-the-time-to

18 http://go.theladders.com/rs/539-NBG-120/images/EyeTracking-Study.pdf

19 https://blog.linkedin.com/2017/march/14/linkedin-profile-photo-tips-introducing-photo-filters-and-

20 https://www.canva.com

21 https://www.canva.com/templates/web-banners/linkedin-banner/

22 https://www.fotor.com

23 http://freelinkedinbackgrounds.com

24 https://pixlr.com/editor/

25 https://blog.linkedin.com/2017/february/17/-tips-for-building-a-great-linkedin-profile-career-expert

26 https://blog.linkedin.com/2018/august/6/make-your-experience-stand-out-with-the-new-linkedin-experience-

27 https://www.statista.com/statistics/264097/number-of-1st-level-connections-of-linkedin-users/

28 https://news.utexas.edu/2014/09/23/looking-for-a-job-having-too-many-contacts-on-linkedin-may-backfire/

29 https://www.linkedin.com/help/linkedin/answer/75814

30 https://blog.linkedin.com/2012/09/20/the-best-way-to-network-with-alumni-on-linkedin

31 https://www.linkedin.com/help/linkedin/answer/52950/commercial-use-limit?lang=en

32 https://www.linkedin.com/help/linkedin/answer/1239?lang=en

33 https://www.truconversion.com/blog/social-media/how-to-create-a-perfect-linkedin-profile/

34 https://images.google.com

35 https://www.linkedin.com/help/linkedin/answer/29

36 https://www.linkedin.com/help/linkedin/answer/2846

37 https://www.linkedin.com/help/linkedin/answer/47081

38 https://blog.linkedin.com/2018/july/26/voice-messaging-on-linkedin-giving-you-more-ways-to-have-conversations

39 https://www.linkedin.com/pulse/why-i-didnt-accept-your-linkedin-request-robert-p-doran

40 https://theessayexpert.com/samples/linkedin-profiles/

41 https://theessayexpert.com/linkedin-profile-summary-distinguish-yourself-from-your-company/

42 https://www.slideshare.net/linkedin/representing-unique-career-paths-on-linkedin

43 https://theessayexpert.com/samples/linkedin-profiles/

44 https://theessayexpert.com/3-reasons-not-to-copy-your-resume-summary-into-your-linkedin-summary-section/

45 https://blog.linkedin.com/2016/05/25/get-comfortable-with-being-uncomfortable-why-now-is-the-time-to

46 https://theessayexpert.com/services-1/resume-and-cover-letter-writing/

47 https://support.grammarly.com/hc/en-us

48 https://www.linkedin.com/in/brendabernstein

49 https://en.wikipedia.org/wiki/List_of_Unicode_characters

50 https://translate.google.com

51 https://theessayexpert.com/samples/linkedin-profiles/

521 https://blog.linkedin.com/2012/12/18/endorse-and-be-endorsed

53 https://getpocket.com

54 https://feedly.com/i/welcome

55 https://www.google.com/alerts

56 https://list.ly

57 https://www.linkedin.com/help/linkedin/answer/34936?lang=en

58 https://www.linkedin.com/help/linkedin/answer/78900

59 https://www.linkedin.com/help/linkedin/answer/85430

60 https://jetpack.com/support/publicize/linkedin/

61 https://blog.linkedin.com/2014/02/19/the-definitive-professional-publishing-platform

62 https://www.linkedin.com/legal/user-agreement

63 https://okdork.com/linkedin-publishing-success/

64 https://www.entrepreneur.com/article/316139

65 https://contentmarketinginstitute.com/2016/08/linkedin-profile-tips/

66 https://www.inc.com/john-white/linkedin-changed-how-they-feature-posts-and-forgot-to-tell-anyone.html

67 https://blog.linkedin.com/2015/04/13/elevate

68 https://www.linkedin.com/help/linkedin/answer/47445?lang=en

69 https://www.entrepreneur.com/article/316139

70 https://blog.linkedin.com/2016/10/12/3-simple-professional-hacks-to-stay-in-the-know-LinkedIn-feed-content

71 https://blog.linkedin.com/2017/march/22/introducing-trending-storylines-discover-trending-news-and-views-on-LinkedIn

72 https://blog.linkedin.com/2017/march/2/simple-tips-to-improve-your-linkedin-feed

73 https://blog.linkedin.com/2018/april/11/make-your-conversations-more-engaging-with-gifs-in-messaging

74 https://www.truconversion.com/blog/social-media/how-to-create-a-perfect-linkedin-profile/

75 https://www.linkedin.com/help/slideshare/answer/61065

76 https://www.forbes.com/sites/kathleenchaykowski/2015/08/25/linkedin-builds-its-education-business-with-new-slideshow-editing-sharing-tool/#72042f470900

77 https://www.linkedin.com/help/linkedin/answer/53685

78 https://blog.linkedin.com/2014/02/06/welcome-bright-to-the-linkedin-family?utm_source=feedburner&utm_medium=email&utm_campaign=Feed%3A+typepad%2Flinkedinblog+%28LinkedIn+Blog%29

79 https://blog.linkedin.com/2016/02/16/offering-hourly-workers-an-opportunity-to-acquire-new-skills-through-snagajob

80 https://www.linkedin.com/learning/

81 https://blog.linkedin.com/2017/october/270/Find-Your-Next-Job-by-Quietly-Signaling-You-are-Open-to-New-Opportunities

82 https://premium.linkedin.com

83 https://www.linkedin.com/help/linkedin/answer/75814

84 https://www.linkedin.com/help/linkedin/answer/70033/viewing-jobs-you-ve-applied-for-on-linkedin

85 https://www.linkedin.com/help/linkedin/answer/71792

86 https://blog.linkedin.com/2018/february/13/introducing-salary-insights-on-jobs

87 https://www.linkedin.com/salary/

88 https://www.wiserutips.com/2013/09/how-and-why-to-follow-companies-on.html

89 https://www.linkedin.com/pulse/new-survey-reveals-85-all-jobs-filled-via-networking-lou-adler/

90 https://business.linkedin.com/talent-solutions/company-career-pages/next-generation-career-pages?

91 https://www.linkedin.com/pulse/how-contact-recruiter-linkedin-breet-chief-stripe-changer

92 https://www.linkedin.com/help/linkedin/answer/166/posting-a-job-on-linkedin?lang=en

93 https://www.linkedin.com/in/lauriejphillips

94 https://www.linkedin.com/in/robinriceconsultant

95 https://www.vault.com/blogs/networking/pros-and-cons-of-linkedin-recommendations-according-to-10-hiring-managers

96 https://blog.linkedin.com/2017/july/12/tuesday-tip-prepare-for-the-day-with-linkedin-calendar-sync

97 https://www.linkedin.com/help/linkedin/answer/50201

98 https://business.linkedin.com/sales-solutions/blog/h/how-sales-reps-exceed-quota-make-club-and-get-promoted-faster

99 https://business.linkedin.com/sales-solutions/blog/g/get-your-score-linkedin-makes-the-social-selling-index-available-for-everyone

100 https://www.linkedin.com/help/linkedin/answer/50191?lang=en

101 https://www.scrubly.com/blog/how-to-mac-contacts/how-to-manually-import-linkedin-contacts-into-mac-contacts/

102 https://smallbiztrends.com/2016/03/average-number-of-social-media-followers-b2b.html

103 https://business.linkedin.com/marketing-solutions/linkedin-pages

104 https://www.forbes.com/sites/williamarruda/2014/01/07/why-every-employee-at-your-company-should-use-linkedin/#7c98f9383c38

105 https://www.linkedin.com/help/linkedin/answer/710

106 https://www.linkedin.com/help/linkedin/answer/44855

107 https://www.linkedin.com/help/linkedin/answer/98740/using-content-suggestions-on-your-linkedin-page

108 https://www.linkedin.com/help/linkedin/answer/1561?lang=en

109 https://business.linkedin.com/marketing-solutions/linkedin-pages/best-practices

110 https://www.linkedin.com/legal/user-agreement

111 https://www.linkedin.com/help/linkedin/answer/544/turning-two-step-verification-on-and-off

112 https://www.linkedin.com/help/linkedin/ask/UAQ

113 https://theessayexpert.com/wp-content/uploads/2018/12/LinkedIn-Profile-Completion-Checklist-2018.pdf

114 https://www.linkedin.com/help/linkedin/answer/190?lang=en

115 https://www.linkedin.com/help/linkedin/answer/71362

116 https://learning.linkedin.com/blog/top-skills/the-skills-companies-need-most-in-2018--and-the-courses-to-get-t

117 https://blog.linkedin.com/2017/january/25/better-than-buzzwords-2017-is-the-year-to-start-showing-it-linkedin

118 https://theessayexpert.com/linkedins-overused-buzzwords-2017-really-need-avoid/

119 https://theessayexpert.com/linkedin-profiles/

120 https://theessayexpert.com/contact/

121 https://university.linkedin.com/linkedin-for-students

122 https://students.linkedin.com

123 https://careers.linkedin.com/students

124 https://blog.linkedin.com/topic/linkedin-for-students

125 https://www.linkedin.com/help/linkedin/answer/61169/linkedin-add-to-profile-feature-frequently-asked-questions?lang=en

126 https://blog.linkedin.com/2015/03/18/add-to-profile

127 https://www.statista.com/statistics/264074/percentage-of-paying-linkedin-users/

128 https://www.linkedin.com/help/linkedin/answer/71?lang=en

129 https://premium.linkedin.com/#premium%20business

130 https://members.linkedin.com/premiumcareer

131 https://business.linkedin.com/talent-solutions

132 https://business.linkedin.com/sales-solutions

133 https://theessayexpert.com/amazon-e-book-update-notifications/

134 https://theessayexpert.com/linkedin-microsoft-resume-assistant-friend-foe/

135 https://www.linkedin.com/help/linkedin/answer/50201

136 https://www.linkedin.com/help/linkedin/answer/1584

137 https://www.linkedin.com/help/linkedin/answer/139

138 https://www.linkedin.com/help/linkedin/answer/71201

139 https://www.linkedin.com/help/linkedin/

140 http://community.linkedin.com/questions/ask.html

141 https://theessayexpert.com/subscribe-to-the-weekly-blog/

142 https://theessayexpert.com/job-search-success-system/

143 https://theessayexpert.com/webinars-podcasts/

144 https://theessayexpert.com/subscribe-to-the-weekly-blog/

145 https://theessayexpert.com/amazon-e-book-update-notifications/

146 https://theessayexpert.com/contact/

147 https://theessayexpert.com/linkedin-profiles/

CPSIA information can be obtained
at www.ICGtesting.com
Printed in the USA
LVHW101551070621
689564LV00006B/381